CHANGING THE GAME

Title IX, Gender, and

College Athletics

OTHER TITLES IN THIS SERIES

Also Available

REACTING TO THE PAST

CHANGING THE GAME

Title IX, Gender, and
College Athletics

Kelly McFall, Newman University
Abigail Perkiss, Kean University

W. W. NORTON & COMPANY
Independent Publishers Since 1923

BARNARD
REACTING TO THE PAST

W. W. Norton & Company has been independent since its founding in 1923, when William Warder Norton and Mary D. Herter Norton first published lectures delivered at the People's Institute, the adult education division of New York City's Cooper Union. The firm soon expanded its program beyond the Institute, publishing books by celebrated academics from America and abroad. By midcentury, the two major pillars of Norton's publishing program—trade books and college texts—were firmly established. In the 1950s, the Norton family transferred control of the company to its employees, and today—with a staff of five hundred and hundreds of trade, college, and professional titles published each year—W. W. Norton & Company stands as the largest and oldest publishing house owned wholly by its employees.

Editor: Justin Cahill
Project Editor: Layne Broadwater
Editorial Assistants: Funto Omojola, Angie Merila
Managing Editor, College: Marian Johnson
Production Manager: Jeremy Burton
Marketing Manager, History: Sarah England Bartley
Design Director: Rubina Yeh
Book Design: Alexandra Charitan
Director of College Permissions: Megan Schindel
Permissions Clearance: Patricia Wong
Photo Editor: Stacey Stambaugh
Composition: Six Red Marbles
Manufacturing: Sheridan books

Permission to use copyrighted material is included in the credits section of this book, which begins on page 169.

ISBN 978-0-393-69666-0

W. Norton & Company, Inc., 500 Fifth Avenue, New York, NY 10110
wwnorton.com
W. W. Norton & Company Ltd., **15 Carlisle Street, London W1D 3BS**

1 2 3 4 5 6 7 8 9 0

ABOUT THE AUTHORS

KELLY McFALL is professor of history and chair of the humanities division at Newman University in Wichita, Kansas. Since 2013, he has run a popular podcast focusing on new books in genocide studies. In 2014, he won the inaugural Faculty of Distinction award from the Kansas Independent College Association, recognizing his teaching excellence. He is a member of the *Reacting to the Past* editorial board and author of a second *Reacting to the Past* game, *The Needs of Others: Human Rights, International Organizations, and Intervention in Rwanda, 1994.*

ABIGAIL PERKISS is assistant professor of history at Kean University in Union, New Jersey. Her first book, *Making Good Neighbors: Civil Rights, Liberalism, and Integration in Postwar Philadelphia* (Cornell University Press, 2014), examined the creation of intentionally integrated neighborhoods in the latter half of the twentieth century. She completed a joint JD/PhD in U.S. history at Temple University. She is the managing and pedagogy editor of the *Oral History Review* and vice president of oral history in the mid-Atlantic region.

CONTENTS

APPENDIX

CHANGING THE GAME

Title IX, Gender, and
College Athletics

PART 1: INTRODUCTION

BRIEF OVERVIEW OF THE GAME

Drive by any YMCA or rec center on a Saturday morning and you'll find fields teeming with kids playing soccer and softball, courts reserved for youth basketball and volleyball, and pools packed with club swim teams. The scenes are commonplace to the point of cliché. The parking lots full of minivans. The trays of sliced oranges. The spectators—moms and dads, uncles and aunts, siblings and friends—filling the bleachers, waiting in anticipation for *their* kid to make the play of the game.

But viewed historically this is not commonplace at all. The idea that girls would want to spend their Saturday morning playing sports would have been almost unthinkable a century ago. And the notion that parents should allow them to do so would have been deeply controversial just a few decades ago. Only the passage of a law called Title IX, and the cultural changes created and fostered by the law, made this modern scene possible.

Changing the Game is about this dramatic change in American society. It asks you to consider the role of women and men in athletics. And it asks you to consider the role of athletics themselves. What does it mean that children spend their weekends on the ball field or that students spend their evenings at games or on the practice field rather than at theater rehearsals or math camp or just playing with friends in the backyard? Is it good that we devote so many resources to sports in our society?

Changing the Game examines both of these sets of issues by plunging students into a debate about the role and cost of athletics at a fictional school, Upper New England University, in the middle of the 1990s.[1] The game begins with debate over the role of athletics at UNEU. But it quickly expands to encompass urgent demands that women's sports receive more resources and female athletes more opportunities. The result is a firestorm of controversy on and off campus. Players debate these pressing issues and propose solutions in a variety of venues, including listening sessions called by the president and student government, talk radio shows, town meetings, and impromptu rallies. The game culminates in a final decision by the University's board of directors.

The game provides a variety of roles for players, including students (some athletes, some not), members of the faculty and administration, residents of the town in which the University is located, members of national lobbying/pressure groups, members of the national media, and donors to/boosters of the University. While many players start the game with their mind already made up, several are unsure what strategy is best. They are available to be convinced by persuasive arguments and lobbying.

Changing the Game is set in the mid-1990s, but the issues it raises are alive and well today. Debate about what it means to make women and men equal hasn't gone away. As the game begins and you take part in the conflict simmering on and off campus at UNEU, you'll encounter questions that are just as relevant nearly three decades later: what does it really mean for men and women to be equal and how should our social institutions play a role in fostering gender equality?

PROLOGUE

*I*t's September in New England—your favorite time of year. Growing up in Tempe, Arizona, you always craved the changing seasons. On TV, winter always had snow, spring was green, summer was hot, and fall . . . well, fall offered crisp air and orange leaves and drinking hot chocolate at football games. With the start of the school year, you can almost taste it. The hint of bite in the air. Plans in the works for the homecoming tailgate.

When you were a kid, you and your dad went to every one of the Arizona State University Sun Devils football games. You were in the crowd in Tucson when they beat the University of Arizona to win the Pac-10 championship in 1986 and were cheering from your living room when they beat Michigan the following month in the Rose Bowl.

But still, watching football in shorts and a T-shirt never felt quite right. You wanted those snowy winters and lush summers. You wanted to go to a game bundled up in three layers, steam misting from your mouth with each breath.

It was one of the things that drew you to Massachusetts when you began looking at colleges; and when you sent in your initial deposit, your first purchase was that bulky hooded sweatshirt, perfect for long hours at the stadium on Saturday afternoons.

First, though, you need to make it through the initial few weeks of junior year.

As part of a project for your history seminar on the civil rights era, you need to interview someone about growing up in the 1950s and 1960s, so last week, you called your mom and asked about her life. You wanted to start with something simple to ease into the conversation, so you asked your mom about her hobbies growing up.

"I took piano lessons from the time I was six or seven years old," she recalled. "And I liked to dance. My friends and I would go to dances every Saturday night. And we watched *American Bandstand* every week. We spent hours and hours dancing and listening to music."

"What about sports?" you asked her. "Were you on any teams in high school?"

"Oh no," she replied, matter-of-factly. "We didn't have any sports teams for girls back then."

"No teams for girls?" you responded.

How could that be?

When you were a kid, all of your friends played sports. Your T-ball team was coed, and for every guy who played Pee Wee football, there was a girl who swam or played soccer or did gymnastics.

You can't imagine anything different.

Your mom opened her high school yearbook, which she had dug out just for the interview. "Well," she said, "we had synchronized swimming. And there were cheer-leaders."

You could hear her leafing through the pages of the old book. She described for you the grainy black-and-white photos of smiling girls in old-fashioned pleated skirts. It sounded like something out of a movie.

"Did you wish it were different?" you asked.

"I was always a really fast runner," she reflected. "If I were your age now, I would join the cross-country team or go out for track. But back then, those teams didn't exist for girls. We didn't really even think about it as a possibility."

After you finished the interview, you hung up the phone and thought about the conversation. You had assumed that your interview would be about the civil rights movement, the women's movement, the Vietnam War—the big events of the time period (and the ones highlighted on your syllabus). But mom was talking about what life was like for regular people, the ones going to school and hanging out with friends and not worrying about politics and war. Being a kid was so different back then.

You felt sorry for your mom, after your talk; you felt bad about all the things she'd missed out on—the experience of being on a team, of that perfect game, even of the epic loss. It's amazing how much has changed, you thought. When you were in high school, your girlfriend was the star point guard on the basketball team. They were one of the top teams in the state, and four of the starting five are playing for Division 1 programs now.

You look down at your watch. Forty minutes until your civil rights era class, just enough time to grab a sandwich and finish up the last of your reading. You walk across the quad and notice a steady stream of people heading toward the Price Auditorium. You don't pay much attention at first; there's always some big lecture taking place. You wave to your buddies from the basketball team. They have a shot at the conference title this year. You were never good enough to play college ball, but your roommate sits on the bench so you've gotten to know some of the guys.

You grab a steak and cheese in the cafeteria and pull out your history textbook. It's loud in here today—everyone seems excited to be back from the break. You feel it too. You had a great summer, but as much as you love your family, by August, you felt ready to get back to your dorm, your friends, and the cute sophomore you just started hanging out with. She's on the swim team, and they're already having informal two-a-day practices, which have her pretty wiped. You brought a video and popcorn to her dorm room last weekend, for a quiet night in.

It's funny how quickly this place has started to feel like home.

You close your history book and pack up. As you make your way over toward class, you look back at the people walking into the auditorium. You notice your history professor hurry through the door. Wait! Don't you have class in ten minutes?

You hustle over to Taylor Hall. When you arrive at your classroom, you see a sign on the door.

> HIST 340 will meet today in the Price Auditorium for a community conversation on the mission of athletics at UNEU.

Huh? What does this have to do with the civil rights movement?

You turn around and walk back toward the auditorium.

And could this talk affect your beloved UNEU football team?

HOW TO REACT

Reacting to the Past is a series of historical role-playing games. Students are given elaborate game books that place them in moments of historical controversy and intellectual ferment. The class becomes a public body of some sort; students, in role, become particular persons from the period, often as members of a faction. Their purpose is to advance a policy agenda and achieve their victory objectives. To do so, they will undertake research and write speeches and position papers; and they will also give formal speeches, participate in informal debates and negotiations, and otherwise work to win the game. After a few preparatory lectures, the game begins, and the players are in charge; the instructor serves as adviser or "gamemaster." Outcomes sometimes differ from the actual history; a postmortem session at the end of the game sets the record straight.

The following is an outline of what you will encounter in Reacting and what you will be expected to do. While these elements are typical of every Reacting game, it is important to remember that every game has its own special quirks.

Game Setup

Your instructor will spend some time before the beginning of the game helping you understand the historical background. During the set-up period, you will read several different kinds of materials, including

- The game book (from which you are reading now), which contains historical information, rules and elements of the game, and essential documents

- Your role sheet, which describes the historical person you will play in the game

You may also be required to read primary and secondary sources outside the game book (perhaps including one or more accompanying books), which provide additional information and arguments for use during the game. Often you will be expected to conduct research to bolster your papers and speeches.

Read all of this contextual material and all of these documents and sources before the game begins. And just as important, go back and reread these materials throughout the game. A second reading while *in role* will deepen your understanding and alter your perspective: ideas take on a different aspect when seen through the eyes of a partisan actor.

Players who have carefully read the materials and who know the rules of the game will invariably do better than those who rely on general impressions and uncertain recollections.

Game Play

Once the game begins, certain players preside over the class sessions. These presiding officers may be elected or appointed. Your instructor then becomes the game-master (GM) and takes a seat in the back of the room. While not in control, the GM may do any of the following:

- Pass notes to spur players to action

- Announce the effects of actions taken inside the game on outside parties (e.g., neighboring countries) or the effects of outside events on game actions (e.g., a declaration of war)

- Interrupt and redirect proceedings that have gone off track

Presiding officers may act in a partisan fashion, speaking in support of particular interests, but they must observe basic standards of fairness. As a failsafe device, most Reacting games employ the "Podium Rule," which allows a player who has not been recognized to approach the podium and wait for a chance to speak. Once at the podium, the player has the floor and must be heard.

To achieve your objectives (outlined in your role sheet) you must persuade others to support you. You must speak with others, because never will a role sheet contain all that you need to know and never will one faction have the strength to prevail without allies. Collaboration and coalition building are at the heart of every game.

Most role descriptions contain secret information you are expected to guard. Exercise caution when discussing your role with others. You may be a member of a faction, which gives you allies who are generally safe and reliable, but even they may not always be in total agreement with you.

In games where factions are tight-knit groups with fixed objectives, finding a persuadable ally can be difficult. Fortunately, every game includes roles that are undecided (or "indeterminate") about certain issues. Everyone is predisposed on certain issues, but most players can be persuaded to support particular positions. Cultivating these players is in your interest. (By contrast, if you are assigned an indeterminate role, you will likely have considerable freedom to choose one or another side in the game; but often, indeterminates have special interests of their own.)

Make friends and find supporters. Before you speak at the podium, arrange to have at least one supporter second your proposal, come to your defense, or admonish those in the body not paying attention. Feel free to ask the presiding officer to assist you, but appeal to the GM only as a last resort.

Immerse yourself in the game. Regard it as a way to escape imaginatively from your usual self—and your customary perspective as a college student in the twenty-first century. At first, this may cause discomfort because you may be advocating ideas that are incompatible with your own beliefs. You may also need to take actions that you would find reprehensible in real life. Remember that a Reacting game is only a game and that you and the other players are merely playing roles. When others offer criticisms, they are not criticizing you as a person. Similarly, you must never criticize another *person* in the game. But you will likely be obliged to criticize their *persona*. (For example, never say, "Sally's argument is ridiculous." But feel free to say, "Governor Winthrop's argument is ridiculous," though you would do well to explain exactly why!) When spoken to by a fellow player—whether in class or out of class—always assume that person is speaking to you in role.

Help create this world by avoiding the colloquialisms and familiarities of today's college life. Remember your role. While a student of the 90s might open a speech with "hi, guys," a dean or trustee would not. Similarly, remember that it is inappropriate to trade on out-of-class relationships when asking for support within the game. ("Hey, you can't vote against me. We're both on the tennis team!")

Reacting to the Past seeks to approximate of the complexity of the past. Because some people in history were not who they seemed to be, so too some roles in Reacting may include elements of conspiracy or deceit. (For example, Brutus did not announce to the Roman Senate his plans to assassinate Caesar.) If you are assigned such a role, you must make it clear to everyone that you are merely playing a role. If, however, you find yourself in a situation where you find your role and actions to be stressful or uncomfortable, tell the GM.

Game Requirements

Your instructor will explain the specific requirements for your class. In general, a Reacting game will require you to perform several distinct but interrelated activities:

- **Reading:** This standard academic work is carried on more purposefully in a Reacting course, since what you read is put to immediate use.

- **Research and Writing:** The exact writing requirements depend on your instructor, but in most cases you will be writing to persuade others. Most of your writing will take the form of policy statements, but you might also write autobiographies, clandestine messages, newspaper articles, or after-game reflections. In most cases, papers are posted on the class website for examination by others. Basic rules: Do not use big fonts or large margins. Do not simply repeat your position as outlined in your role sheet; you must base your arguments on historical facts as well as ideas drawn from assigned texts, and from independent research. (Your instructor will outline the requirements for footnoting and attribution.) Be sure to consider the weaknesses in your argument and address them; if you do not, your opponents will.

- **Public Speaking and Debate:** Most players are expected to deliver at least one formal speech from the podium (the length of the game and the size of the class will affect the number of speeches). Reading papers aloud is seldom effective. Some instructors may insist that students instead speak freely from notes. After a speech, a lively and even raucous debate will likely ensue. Often the debates will culminate in a vote.

- **Strategizing:** Communication among students is a pervasive feature of Reacting games. You should find yourself writing emails, texting, and attending meetings on a fairly regular basis. If you do not, you are being outmaneuvered by your opponents.

Skill Development

A recent Associated Press article on education and employment made the following observations:

> The world's top employers are pickier than ever. And they want to see more than high marks and the right degree. They want graduates with so-called soft skills—those who can work well in teams, write and speak with clarity, adapt quickly to changes in technology and business conditions, and interact with colleagues from different countries and cultures. . . . And companies are going to ever-greater lengths to identify the students who have the right mix of skills, by observing them in role-playing exercises to see how they handle pressure and get along with others . . . and [by] organizing contests that reveal how students solve problems and handle deadline pressure.

Reacting to the Past, probably better than most elements of the curriculum, provides the opportunity for developing these "soft skills." This is because you will be practicing persuasive writing, public speaking, critical thinking, problem solving, and collaboration. You will also need to adapt to changing circumstances and work under pressure.

 PART 2: HISTORICAL BACKGROUND

CHRONOLOGY

1964	The Civil Rights Act of 1964 prohibits discrimination in employment based on race, sex, national origin, or religion
1966	National Organization of Women (NOW) founded with the mission of ending gender-based discrimination
1972	Title IX passed and signed into law
1975	Department of Health, Education, and Welfare (HEW) issues guidelines for evaluating compliance with Title IX
1978	Year by which high schools and postsecondary institutions obliged to be in compliance with Title IX
1979	HEW issues interpretation on Title IX compliance (three-pronged test)
1979	ESPN began broadcasting
1984	In *Gove City College v. Bell*, U.S. Supreme Court holds that only programs that receive direct federal financial aid must comply with Title IX
1988	Congress passes the Civil Rights Restoration Act, requiring programs receiving indirect aid to comply with Title IX
1992	U.S. Supreme Court allows monetary damages in Title IX lawsuits in *Franklin v. Gwinnett County Schools*
1993	U.S. Supreme Court rules that schools may not use budget challenges as an excuse to avoid Title IX in *Favia v. Indiana University of Pennsylvania*
1994	Federal prosecutors indict University of Miami academic adviser Tony Russell on charges of falsifying Pell Grant applications for eighty-five student-athletes. That same year, the *Miami Herald* reports that boosters for the school's football team set up a pay-for-play program, offering financial compensation to players for good stats on the field
1995	House Subcommittee on Postsecondary Education holds hearings on Title IX
1995–96	University of Massachusetts basketball team reaches the Final Four, led by star player Marcus Camby

SPORTS, GENDER, AND EQUALITY: THE ORIGINS OF TITLE IX

The history of women in sports is one marred by waves of exclusion and discrimination, but it is also marked by moments of celebration, empowerment, and the creation of alternate spaces for competition. In 776 B.C.E., for example, women were excluded from the first Olympic Games in the Greek republic. In response, they developed the Games of Hera (or Heraean Games), an all-female athletic competition named in tribute to the Greek goddess of women. More than two millennia later, when the Olympics were reincarnated in 1896 in their modern guise, Charles Pierre de Frédy, Baron de Coubertin, the founder of the International Olympic Committee, famously argued that including women would be "impractical, uninteresting, unaesthetic, and incorrect." Yet the eighteenth and nineteenth centuries saw the emergence of a small cadre of elite women breaking barriers in the worlds of sports and competition. In 1722, British boxer Elizabeth Wilkinson entered the ring for the first time. In 1804, Alicia Meynell of England became the first known female jockey to compete in horse racing. In 1866, Vassar College, which opened its doors a year earlier as an all-women's school, founded the first amateur women's basketball team in the United States.

A century later, as you'll read later, in the United States and around the world, women were breaking down barriers in the workplace, the legal system, and the bedroom. In the early 1970s, they successfully pushed for change in higher education as well. With the passage of Title IX of the Education Amendments of 1972, federally funded educational institutions were forbidden from discriminating against students or employees on the basis of their sex.

> No person in the United States shall, on the basis of sex, be excluded from participation in, be denied the benefits of, or be subjected to discrimination under any education program or activity receiving Federal financial assistance.

Title IX created the first federally mandated proscription on gender inequality in education. The law had particular resonance in the realm of athletics. Suddenly, schools were required to proactively create new opportunities for women in sports and work to enforce equal access and equal quality to these new athletes. It also set the stage for decades of uncertainty and contentiousness, as courts worked to interpret the law and individual schools tried to balance compliance with the very tangible realities of limited budgets, competing institutional interests, and pushback from men's programs worried about losing their own resources and standing.

How did we get to that point?

The Emergence of Modern Sports in Europe

While sports and competition date back to the earliest of human interactions, historians trace the development of modern sports to the eighteenth century. The emergence of organized sports was born out of the Enlightenment period in Europe, as democratizing impulses created the space for people of all social classes to mingle and interact as relative equals.[1] The establishment of this new public domain set the groundwork for new social opportunities outside of the family structure. These associations took the form of coffeehouses, the press, and public societies, and—most notably—sports clubs.

At first, these recreational activities were exclusively available to the elite, but society was changing quickly. A period of technological innovation, what we now call the **Industrial Revolution**, brought efficiencies to agricultural production with tools like the cotton gin and the power loom. At the same time, governments began enacting legislation to create more humane work conditions for the labor class. In Britain, for instance, Parliament passed the Ten Hours Act in 1847, which created caps on the workday for youth and women in factories. Three years later, the Factory Act of 1850 imposed such limitations for all industrial workers. This combination of increasing productivity and constraints on work hours meant that people across all economic classes now had more leisure time. In turn, it created the space for an increased focus on sports and recreation. At the same time, the growth of the railroad expanded access to fields and tracks, bringing access to both watching and playing sports to people across the country. The same was true across Europe.

The **Industrial Revolution** marked the transition from an economic system grounded in farming and agriculture to one built on manufacturing and production. It describes a period from the mid-eighteenth century and the early nineteenth century characterized by urbanization and widespread population growth.

Organized scholastic sports as we now understand them first emerged in the nineteenth century in Britain's elite public schools.[2] There, sports came to be viewed as a critical part of the educational experience, write historians C. Roger Rees and Andrew Miracle, because "of their 'character building' properties." These athletic experiences, especially team sports, were meant to imbue students with a sense of "group loyalty, physical toughness, and self-reliance."[3]

At first, this new focus on sports and leisure was concentrated in Europe, but with colonial expansion—as European nations asserted their reach and authority over parts of Africa, Asia, and Latin America—organized competition quickly spread across the globe. In 1896, the first modern Olympic Games were held in Athens, Greece. The event, a revival of the religious and athletic festivals held every four years in ancient Greece, brought together more than 200 athletes, all men, from fourteen countries to compete in such sports as cycling, swimming, wrestling, and tennis. Four years later, women were invited to take part. In the 1900 games, held in Paris, France, twenty-two female athletes competed, 2.2 percent of the total field. Their participation was limited to sailing, lawn tennis, golf, and croquet (the only time the sport was included in the Olympic Games, for men or women).

The Development of Sports in the United States

The rise of organized sports emerged in the United States amid these same social and economic conditions: increased efficiency in production, reforms in labor laws, and democratizing trends in recreational opportunities. Regional differences persisted through the late nineteenth century, with baseball gaining popularity in the northeast and American football developing throughout the southeast. It wasn't until the end of the Civil War that a national culture of sports began to grow, around the same time that a broader sense of nationhood took hold.

This emergence of recreational sports and the attendant development of amateur sports organizations led to new opportunities and the growing popularity of sports in the United States at large. The New York Knickerbockers, founded in 1845 by Alexander Cartwright as a social club for men of "distinguished economic and social status," is said to be the first amateur athletic organization in the United States. The group created a set of formal rules to govern competition and established a recreational baseball league throughout New York City. Nearly half a century later, in 1888, William Buckingham Curtis, a longtime advocate for organized sports, founded the Amateur Athletic Union (AAU), which would go on to become one of the largest voluntary sports organizations in the nation. Meanwhile, intercollegiate sports competition for men began in 1852, when the Harvard and Yale rowing clubs faced off in a 3.2-kilometer race on New Hampshire's Lake Winnipesaukee. Harvard's first boat took the top prize—a pair of black walnut trophy oars—but charges soon emerged that the team had brought in a ringer in the coxswain seat.

For much of this time, women were confined to recreational activities that required only modest physical exertion. Few challenged such restrictions, because of a widely held belief that too much activity could be dangerous for "the fairer sex," who were viewed as weak and in need of protection. But by the late nineteenth century, agitation for women's participation in athletics reached a critical mass. The change is linked to two parallel developments. First, the advent of the "safety bicycle," so called because the riders feet could reach the ground, offered unprecedented opportunities for women to incorporate activity into their daily lives and experience the new freedoms afforded by their own means of transportation.[4]

At the same time, women began to reject certain notions of gender that had become established in the United States and Europe during the reign of Queen Victoria (these norms are often called Victorian morality). The most powerful of these ideas was that women's place was in the domestic sphere and that only men should have legal rights to vote or hold property. But by the early 1900s, some women began to insist that these social and legal norms were restrictive. This post-Victorian era gave way to heightened cries for women's equality and suffrage and also to a sense that women could and should participate in pursuits outside of their home and family life, including physical activity.

THE "NEW WOMAN" AND HER BICYCLE.——THERE WILL BE SEVERAL VARIETIES OF HER.

These two shifts, cultural and technological, can be seen as mutually rein-forcing. The advent of the bicycle prompted new trends in women's clothing, as designers began to respond to the need for more freedom of movement by removing corsets from dresses and developing women's cycling bloomers and trousers (these, of course, were met with derision by some segments of society).[5] At the same time, changing notions of gender and identity prompted women to seek out activity as a marker of their newfound social freedom. As suffragist Susan B. Anthony wrote in 1896, "bicycling has done more to emancipate women than anything else in the world. I stand and rejoice every time I see a woman ride on a wheel. It gives women a feeling of freedom and self-reliance." This intersec-tion, then, created the space for women, for the first time in large numbers, to begin to enter the athletic sphere.

Sports also came to be seen as a way to instill the Protestant ethic of hard work in America's youth. According to historian Robert Halpern, progressive reformers in the early twentieth century believed that athletics could cure social ills such as urban overcrowding and economic vulnerability by preparing children for the emerging industrial society in the United States. As the **Progressive Era** saw the creation of several organizations aimed at remedying the ills caused by a rapidly changing society, this period also gave way to the creation of youth athletic leagues in urban areas across the coun-try, designed to instill youth with an ethos of "the 'American' values of cooperation, hard work, and respect for authority."[6] These organizations created the space for formal competition for boys, starting as school-sponsored leagues and expanding to community clubs.

The **Progressive Era** refers to a period of widespread political reform in the United States from the late nineteenth to early twentieth centuries. Reformers aimed to solve what they saw as the ill effects of urbanization and immigration and to take on the entrenched political corruption in cities across the nation.

The first intercollegiate competition for women came on April 4, 1896, when the University of California, Berkeley's women's basketball team faced off against Stanford at San Francisco's Page Street Armory. More than 700 fans attended—all women, because men had been banned from the arena to protect the modesty of the players. By the early 1900s, popular magazines had proclaimed the creation of "the modern athletic girl."[7] These women were seen as independent, emancipated, and empowered. Female athletes became celebrities, and young girls sought to emulate them. And as more women were introduced to athletics, they quickly became more competitive as well.[8] In the 1920s, the National Amateur Athletic Foundation (NAAF) established a women's division. That same decade, the AAU held national championships for women's track, basketball, and swimming, and the Olympic Games opened up competition in skating, swimming and diving, and track and field.[9]

Still, criticism persisted. Opponents warned that women's purity would be corrupted by the introduction of competition, that their femininity would be compromised, and that their health would be jeopardized by such taxing physical exertion. "They'll ruin their reproductive organs," detractors cautioned. "They're risking injury, emotional and mental collapse, sexual indecency."[10] Athletes withstood charges of threatening existing family structures, of homosexuality, and of radicalism. Three years after that first intercollegiate game, Stanford canceled its women's basketball program, according to the faculty, "for the good of the students' health."[11]

While opportunities for physical education and recreation expanded for girls and young women, such criticism had the effect of limiting opportunities for athletic competition. The NAAF's women's division served as one of the key enforcers for these limitations, highlighting the need for "play for play's sake" and instituting restrictions on awards and travel. This philosophy had the effect of limiting opportunities for competition and curtailing financial support. As was the case with Stanford's basketball program, such policies and practices slowed the growth of collegiate athletic opportunities for women across the country, and competitive sports for college women decreased across the board.[12]

Regulation and the NCAA

As women's athletic competition fell under attack, men's athletic pursuits were becoming increasingly regulated, particularly at the university level. Throughout the latter half of the nineteenth century, collegiate sports ballooned. Sometimes with the support of their institutions, and often through the creation of informal athletic associations, outside of the bounds of administrative oversight, students across the country were organizing sporting events, cultivating teams, and selling tickets. Administrators grew concerned. In 1873, Cornell University president Andrew Dickson White sent a telegram to officials at the University of Michigan regarding an upcoming football game between the two schools: "I will not permit thirty men to travel four hundred miles merely to agitate a bag of wind."[13] In the late nineteenth century, MIT president Francis Walker lamented, "If the movement [away from a focus on academics] shall continue at this same rate, it will soon be fairly a question whether the letters B.A. stand more for Bachelor of Arts or Bachelor of Athletics."[14]

Increasing concerns over player safety compounded these worries. The 1905 football season, dubbed the "death harvest" by the *Chicago Tribune*, saw eighteen students killed and more than one hundred injured in intercollegiate play. The carnage prompted President Theodore Roosevelt, whose own son had recently joined Harvard's freshman football team and had already suffered a broken nose in a game against Yale, to convene two White House conferences to address the need for reform in collegiate athletics. Out of those meetings, the Intercollegiate Athletic Association of the United States—renamed the National Collegiate Athletic Association (NCAA) in 1910—was born.

Early on, the NCAA provided only modest oversight in intercollegiate sports. At its inception, it took on the role of establishing a set of rules and regulations for university athletics, most notably football. A decade after its founding, the organization hosted the first national collegiate championship events, starting with track and field in 1921. But as athletics became a fundamental part of college life and culture, the NCAA began to assert increasing control over the rules and regulations governing competition, aiming to limit growing efforts from universities to bring in revenue from college sports and assuage growing pressures on athletes to prioritize sports over the academic and social experiences of university life.

The link between athletics and capitalism was not new. Betting on athletic competitions dates back to the eighteenth century. In the mid-nineteenth century, amateur baseball teams began charging for admission to their games and dividing the proceeds among the players. The first recognized professional team in the country was the Cincinnati Red Stockings, a member of the National Association of Base Ball Players, the nation's first amateur baseball league. The Red Stockings first began compensating players in 1867, and by 1869, they had an entirely professional roster. Two years later, the league itself declared professional status and began collecting a cut of the profits as well. In 1887, a parallel professional league emerged, reflecting the segregationist culture and social structure in the United States. This National Colored Base Ball League brought together eight teams in the Mid-Atlantic region and created an organizational structure for African American professional sports. Though the league folded that same year, it paved the way for subsequent all-black sports associations, culminating in the Negro National League, which ran from 1920 to 1932.

Despite the growth of professionalized sports in the early decades of the twentieth century, the growing link between money and *college* athletics troubled many. In a 1929 report, the Carnegie Foundation for the Advancement of Teaching, an education policy and research center in the United States, warned that collegiate sports programs had transformed from amateur competition to "highly profitable enterprises." College sports, wrote Henry Pritchett, president of the foundation, in the report's preface, "have been developed from games played by boys for pleasure into systematic professionalized athletic contests for the glory and, too often, for the financial profit for the college."[15] The report criticized a culture that turned students into commodities and thrust them into the public spotlight as promotional ads for the schools. It advocated for a renewed emphasis on the character-building role of athletics and a disavowal of the commercial focus.

The same year that the Carnegie report was published, the stock market crash of 1929 touched off a brewing economic collapse in the United States and around the world. The **Great Depression** had profound effects on every aspect of American life, including athletics. During the 1930s, many amateur athletic clubs shut their doors, limiting access to organized sports to those who could afford it. Groups like the Young Men's Christian Association (YMCA) began charging fees for participation, closing off opportunities for children in poorer communities and creating an income gap in recreational activities that would continue to grow through the twentieth century.[16]

The **Great Depression** refers to the global economic downturn of the 1930s. In the United States, specifically, the period is characterized by widespread unemployment; environmental vulnerabilities, including the Dust Bowl; and significant political reform, including a reimagination of the relationship between government and the American people.

Ironically, the collapse of the U.S. economy in the 1930s also created more athletic opportunities for women, as financial need destabilized traditional gender roles and allowed for the possibility of women entering public life in new ways. In the 1930s, Mildred Burke and Billy Wolfe, recognizing that there was profit to be made from women in sports, established women's professional wrestling in the United States. What began as a carnival act in which Burke would wrestle men for spectacle turned into a highly lucrative women's league (and, briefly, a highly volatile marriage). Though largely staged, the endeavor spanned two decades and was recognized by the National Wrestling Alliance. Burke, herself, competed in five thousand matches in the United States and Japan, without a single loss.[17]

A decade later, the onset of World War II further catapulted women into the arena of professional sports. As scores of male athletes enlisted in the military and shipped off to fight overseas, industrious executives at Major League Baseball created a parallel women's league to fill the void left by their absence on the field and maintaining the presence of baseball in American life during the war. The All-American Girls Professional Baseball League kicked off its inaugural season on May 30, 1943, with sixty women on the roster. Over the next eleven years, the lifespan of the league, more than six hundred salaried women would compete on fifteen teams throughout the Midwest.

At the collegiate level, the Depression led to dramatic dips in enrollment at American universities, briefly quieting conversations about athletic commercialization and regulation. In the wake of World War II, however, new federal benefits programs for veterans, coupled with a push for educational desegregation, led to a swelling of student body populations at colleges and universities across the country. At the same time, the emergence and growth of mass media brought with it increasing exposure for college athletics and, as such, increasing interest from both fan bases and participants alike. These new conditions prompted renewed calls for regulation on the part of the NCAA: new rules, expanded governance, and ever-increasing oversight.

At the same time, athletic prowess became a marker of geopolitical success in the escalating conflict between the United States and the Soviet Union—the Cold War. The 1952 Olympics, the first that included Russian athletes since 1912, was rivaled only by the space race in the fight for the "free world." During the post-war era a culture of conformity pervaded American society, including a return to traditional gender expectations and family structures.[18] This conservative turn served to restrict women's participation in life outside of the home, including employment, education, and athletics, and to threaten their inclusion in competitive sports.

The beginning of the Cold War also forced the country to think about its international image in new ways. The United States and the Soviet Union were vying for power across the globe, and these battles were particularly heated in small non-allied nations. The Truman administration realized that it was in the nation's best interest to pursue an agenda of racial progress because doing so legitimated U.S. claims of democratic promise. And, gradually, these efforts toward racial equality gave way to renewed calls for gender equality.

While early feminist activism was directed toward women's suffrage and legal equality, this second wave feminism of the 1960s and 1970s focused, in part, on overcoming de facto inequality in the public sphere: in the workplace, political life, and education. And with the push for expanded access and autonomy came increasing efforts for inclusion in organized athletics.

The Fight for Inclusion

Though women's intercollegiate athletics had existed since the 1896 Stanford–Berkeley basketball game and had been organized nationally since 1941 with the first collegiate golf championship, it wasn't until the 1970s that the United States saw widespread support for a nationally organized system of women's collegiate sports. In 1963, the American Alliance for Health, Physical Education, and Recreation—then the governing body for many types of recreational programs for women—changed its longstanding policy against intercollegiate women's athletics. Three years later, the organization created a commission that would become in 1971 the Association for Intercollegiate Athletics for Women, or AIAW. This group was charged with assisting in the creation of formalized leagues for women's college sports. In the years to follow, the AIAW held national championships for women's gymnastics, track, swimming, badminton, basketball, and volleyball. The organization saw sports as a vehicle for education and character building for female student-athletes. In its first year in existence, 278 universities joined the AIAW; within a decade, membership increased to 800.

This period also saw a rise in women's athletics in the larger public sphere. In 1966, college student Roberta Gibb became the first woman to run the Boston Marathon. The Boston Athletic Association had rejected her application for a formal race number because the Amateur Athletic Union, which sanctioned the event, prohibited women from racing more than 1.5 miles. So, the Massachusetts native ran unsanctioned. At the beginning of the race, Gibb, clad in a black bathing suit, a hooded sweatshirt, and her brother's Bermuda shorts, hid in the bushes. When half of the 415 competing runners crossed the start line, she quietly slipped into the crowd. The men on the course were supportive, and she talked easily with the runners around her. When she tossed her sweatshirt at mile 2, the press began to pick up the story. Word traveled fast. By the time she passed the all-women's Wellesley College at mile 12, students were lining the street. "I could hear them a half mile away," Gibb said. "In those days, there was limited security, so the girls ran out into the road and raised their arms to form a tunnel that we ran through. . . . The sound was deafening."[19] At three hours, twenty-one minutes, and forty seconds after she began, Gibb crossed the finish line at Copley Square. She had beaten more than two-thirds of the field.

Though Gibb's unsanctioned run garnered widespread support from the public and local officials and though journalists around the country celebrated the historic run, Boston Marathon officials at first took a hard line, refusing to change the rules of entry. The following year, Katherine Switzer, who was misidentified as a man and granted a race number when she registered with only her initials, was greeted with jeers and violence on the course. It wasn't until 1972 that the AAU finally created a women's division for the marathon distance.

A year later, tennis star Billie Jean King defeated former world champion Bobby Riggs in the now-famed Battle of the Sexes. Riggs, fifty-five years old and by then known better for his showboating than his tennis prowess, boasted that he could beat any of the top women's players. King, ranked second in the world that year, initially dismissed Riggs's challenge. But his persistence (coupled with a victory over number one ranked Margaret Court) ultimately was rewarded when King agreed to an exhibition match with a winning prize purse of $100,000. The event drew more than thirty thousand spectators to the Houston Astrodome. Ninety million more watched on television as King paraded into the arena on a platform carried by four men dressed as ancient Egyptian slaves. Riggs followed in a rickshaw, wearing a jacket emblazoned with the Sugar Daddy candy logo. The game itself was short and unceremonious—King defeated Riggs in three straight sets and just over two hours—but the reverberations were profound. To the world, the match signaled widespread shifts in women's place in the world of sports.

Perhaps no image better represents this shift than the iconic photo on the cover of this book. On February 22, 1975, Madison Square Garden played host to the first women's college basketball game in the history of the arena. That afternoon, Immaculata College and their famed Mighty Macs defeated Queens College, 65–61, before more than 12,000 spectators. The game was a rematch of the 1973 AIAW championship final, and the stakes were high for both teams. For the world of women's athletics, the consequences were even higher. "It was a defining moment for women's basketball and for women in general," recalled freshman guard Donna Orender, who went on to become president of the WNBA. "I can still hear Helen Reddy singing 'I am woman, hear me roar.' The crowd was screaming, and tears rolled down my cheeks on the layup line."[20] The iconic Immaculata/Queen's game would later be credited for the growth of women's collegiate basketball around the country.

The Passage of Title IX

The shift of women into sports wasn't only a cultural phenomenon; it was officially codified into law with the passage of Title IX of the Higher Education Amendments of 1972. Drafted by Congresswoman Patsy Mink, the legislation prohibited the restriction of educational opportunities based on sex. Title IX was, in a sense, a response to Title VI of the Civil Rights Act of 1964, which forbade discrimination in federally assisted programs, including education, on the basis of race, color, national origin, or religion—but not sex. With the passage of Title IX eight years later, gender-based discrimination had finally received the same recognition. The law had the effect of ushering in a new era of women's sports across the nation.

When President Nixon signed the bill into law, he charged the Department of Health, Education, and Welfare (HEW) with overseeing the implementation of the new policies at individual institutions of higher learning. The first challenge to the legislation came two years later, when Senator John Tower put forward an amendment to exempt revenue-producing sports like football where all participants, of course, were men from Title IX compliance. Though the proposal was ultimately struck down, soon after Congress adopted the Javits Amendment, which mandated that HEW consider and include "reasonable provisions" relevant to the nature of each individual sport in executing Title IX policies. The amendment was interpreted to mean that equity, or fairness, did not necessarily require parity or sameness. So, for example, equipment costs for individual sports could be allocated based on perceived need, rather than the idea that each sport must be allocated equivalent funds.[21]

At the time it was passed, Title IX received little fanfare. It was tucked into a lengthy piece of legislation that outlined broad regulations for institutional conduct in all realms of higher education. But questions began to emerge. Would funding for men's teams disappear? Would teams be cut? Would scholarships be taken away? This catapulted the Title IX provision into the national spotlight, where its intent and application would be intensely debated.

In 1979, seven years after Title IX was enacted and five years after the Javits Amendment was passed, HEW issued a final policy interpretation on the law, laying out a three-pronged test to verify Title IX compliance. The HEW test mandated that schools must meet one of the following three standards to be found in compliance of Title IX:

1. The number of athletes from each sex at a school must be roughly equivalent to enrollment percentages, or

2. A school must demonstrate a history and continuing practice of expanding athletic opportunities for the underrepresented sex (most commonly, women), or

3. A school must show that the interests and abilities of female athletes are being fully and effectively accommodated.

This test set the stage for decades of wrangling, as institutions and courts worked to negotiate the complicated relationship between gender equity, resource allocation, and representation in college athletics.

The first Supreme Court case to directly address the reach and scope of Title IX came that same year. In *Cannon v. University of Chicago* (1979), Justice John Stevens, writing for the majority, ruled that a woman could sue the University of Chicago for a denial of admittance to medical school on the basis of her sex. More broadly, the court held, individuals have the right to sue a school for discriminatory policies in violation of Title IX. The case became the foundation for dozens of lawsuits in the years to follow.

Five years later, in *Grove City College v. Bell* (1984), the Court restricted the reach of the law. While Title IX applies even to private universities where a substantial number of students receive federal aid, wrote Justice Byron White, the legislation applies only to how an institution allocates its financial aid and not to how it administers its athletic programs. The ruling effectively ended the statute's application to intercollegiate athletic programs beyond the regulation of athletic scholarships.

These restrictions were short lived. In March 1988, the Civil Rights Restoration Act was passed, mandating that Title IX be applied to *all* operations of any school receiving such funds, overturning *Grove City College* and reaffirming the relevance of Title IX in all aspects of college life, including sports. Four years later, the court added more teeth to the law, when it held in *Franklin v. Gwinnett County Public Schools* (1992) that punitive damages be awarded when schools intentionally avoid Title IX compliance.

Implementing Title IX: A Fight for Control

As debates over the enforcement of Title IX wended their way through state and federal courts, universities and intercollegiate associations grappled with how to interpret and implement the law on the ground. The NCAA at first issued sharp criticism of the legislation, arguing that it would have the effect of undercutting men's sports. But the growth of women's sports meant the potential for increased revenue for universities and intercollegiate associations, and that money proved a powerful incentive for the NCAA to expand its purview. This profit incentive was especially powerful during a time of national economic stagnation, when the association itself was instituting cost control measures and concerned to preserve its viability. At a 1975 special convention, NCAA president Walter Byers noted, "It is probably better to cut off the hand than to die."[22]

By the late 1970s, the association seriously considered the creation of a women's division, and in 1981, leadership passed a comprehensive plan for the creation of a women's sports program, including allocating four slots on their council to women and creating the framework for women's championship events nationwide.

Because the NCAA until the early 1980s operated almost exclusively to oversee men's athletics programs, it was the AIAW that served as the voice for women's intercollegiate athletics in the United States.[23] As it had before the passage of Title IX, the organization continued to emphasize the role of sports in fostering community, improving academic outcomes, and empowering female athletes, often minimizing the focus on competition itself. And women's collegiate athletics grew—enough, by the early 1980s, to sustain forty-one national championships in nineteen sports, all under their auspices of the AIAW.

That fall, collegiate programs were permitted to compete in both NCAA and AIAW tournaments, but soon schools were pressured to support one association or the other. The resources and exposure offered by the NCAA were hard for universities to ignore. In 1983, following a year-long legal battle during which the AIAW charged the NCAA with institutional corruption, commodifying collegiate athletes, and disregarding their academic interests, the AIAW disbanded, leaving the NCAA as the sole arbiter of national intercollegiate athletics, for men *and* women.

DISTRIBUTIVE JUSTICE: TOWARD A THEORY OF COMPLIANCE

At the core of many of these debates surrounding Title IX—how resources would be allocated among sports programs, whether men's programs would be cut— were deeper philosophical questions about the ways we mitigate injustice and implement change in society. How do we repair past wrongs? How do we fairly allocate resources among diverse groups and community members?

During the first fifteen years after the passage of Title IX, many schools were able to sidestep the question of distribution because of the U.S. Supreme Court's narrow interpretation of the reach of the law, culminating in the *Grove City College* decision. But when the Court held in 1988 that the Civil Rights Restoration Act mandated the application of Title IX to all programs at schools receiving federal funding, a new class of cases emerged, forcing a more nuanced understanding of the law and its application. Suddenly, it wasn't simply a matter of how federal aid money was distributed to male and female students, but whether federally supported institutions offered equitable programming. These court cases, coming from both male and female athletes, pushed courts to confront the distribution of resources in new ways.

This new period of Title IX challenges coincided with an economic downturn, a period when finances at many schools were constricted, often including substantial cuts to athletics. Such retrenchment meant that it wasn't always possible simply to *expand* the budget to include more resources for women's athletics. Rather, as women agitated for more support, men's programs were also seeing cutbacks and, in some cases, elimination. This was particularly true for non-revenue-generating programs. Between 1981 and 1999, for instance, more than 170 men's varsity wrestling programs were cut around the country.[24] These cutbacks weren't unilateral or the direct result of a Title IX mandate but rather were the result of individual institutions working to manage limited university resources, given many competing interests and priorities. In fact, during that same period, more than a hundred women's gymnastics programs lost their funding as well. Even so, many came to view Title IX as the central villain in an oversimplified story that pitted female athletes advocating for greater representation against male athletes protesting the withdrawal of resources from their programs.

As frustration grew from male and female athletes alike, those implementing and administering Title IX sought a better understanding for how to allocate resources in accordance with the law. Therein lay the need for a consensus theory of *distributive justice*. From its passage, courts, advocacy groups, and even universities relied on this notion in their discussion and application of Title IX. Political theorist Chris Armstrong describes distributive justice as a mechanism through which to fairly allocate resources, a principle, he says, "which tells us how some particular benefit or burden *ought* to be shared out."[25] But, of course, fairness is contestable, and as institutions tried to remedy past injustices, those who benefited from them often felt "wronged" in the righting. As philosopher Michelle Maiese writes, "redistribution always has losers, and they often initiate a conflict of their own."[26] Thus the challenge of distributive justice is to find the most materially fair allocation for everyone involved.

There are five generally agreed on theories of distributive justice, each offering a different vision of how to most effectively allocate resources:

- **The Equity Principle:** Outcome should be based on input—that is, when an individual invests substantial resources, that person should benefit more than someone who has contributed very little.

- **The Equality Principle:** All members of a particular group should receive an equal share, regardless of input.

- **The Power Principle:** Those individuals who hold more status or power should receive more than those with lower status or power.

- **The Need Principle:** Those with the greatest need should have their needs met.

- **The Responsibility Principle:** Those who have the most should share their resources with those who do not.

Before the implementation of Title IX, the goods and services derived from intercollegiate athletics—scholarships, travel, training facilities, equipment and kit, recognition, meals, and so on—were distributed largely to male athletes. With the passage of the law, though, female athletes became entitled to their share of these goods. But what was their fair share? How should we determine allocation of those resources? Which theory of distributive justice should be applied?

Early on, as noted earlier, the limited reach of Title IX offered an easy work-around on this question. But in the post-1988 era, after the passage of the Civil Rights Restoration Act, courts came to rely on a balance of the *need* and *equity* approaches to distributive justice in applying the HEW's three-pronged test. This position, philosopher Leslie Francis suggests, "reflects an uneasy compromise between exactly equal levels of participation and the historical differences between men's and women's sports."[27] This approach allowed for and accepted widespread disparities at the individual program level—for instance, the continuation of football programs that dominate university athletic resources, so long as the institution can provide sufficient evidence of overall proportional representation and resources across the athletic programs.

Many have criticized this practice of proportionality. First, these critics argue, such an approach decreases opportunities for male athletes in non-revenue-generating sports. They cite the elimination of dozens of men's wrestling, tennis, gymnastics, swimming, and golf programs as substantial evidence of the subjugation of men's athletics over women's.[28]

Others suggest that the proportionality requirement masks important moral questions about the role and purpose of collegiate athletic programs. Proponents of university athletics generally tout the value of the athletics programs for both the school and the individual athletes. They suggest that athletics creates a source of upward mobility for disadvantaged students, that sports programs boost self-esteem, and that successful programs create cohesive identities for the university community and benefit the school with greater alumni donations, stronger admission candidates, and more respect nationwide. Critics, however, point to studies suggesting that some schools have privileged athletics programs and facilities over academic interests and that graduation rates for athletes, particularly minority athletes in football and basketball, are substantially lower than the rates of the overall student population.

Some detractors use these data to propose the answer to gender inequity in collegiate athletics may be to disinvest from athletic programs overall. According to philosopher Robert Simon, Title IX advocates base their work on the presumption that to deny access by gender is unjust. However, writes Simon, "it doesn't follow from this that educational institutions, particularly colleges and universities, should support athletic teams and engage in the existing practice of intercollegiate sport. Whether colleges and universities ought to support intercollegiate athletics in the first place is a different issue from what counts as gender equity once such programs are already established."[29] The case could be made, argues Francis, for universities to take the "radical" approach of rethinking their current athletics programs more broadly.[30] And this debate points to another fundamental question: What is the role and function of a college or university?

HOW DOES A UNIVERSITY WORK?

Students often know a lot about specific aspects of life at a university: where to go to get an ID card, where to find out where their adviser's office is, where to change their schedule, etc. But universities are complicated places, and the things you know may not be the kinds of things that you need to know to play this Reacting game. The following, then, is a very brief introduction to some of the ways universities make policies and decisions, limited largely to the issues and areas relevant to *Changing the Game*.

Every university is governed by a board of directors, which has overall authority over the institution.[31] The board is usually between ten and fifteen people and meets quarterly to monitor the university's progress; to revise, add, or eliminate programs; and to review policies. It can also come together for exceptional emergency meetings to address specific questions or challenges. The board is run by a chair, who sets the agenda and runs the meeting.

Generally speaking, a university's board of directors serves two central functions. First, it works to ensure the university continues to exist and that it remains focused on achieving the mission laid out for the institution. Accordingly, it supervises and approves the budget, both to make sure the school spends responsibly and to fund programs and positions that best fit the overall vision for the niche the university will fill in the world of higher education. In addition, it has overall authority over policies ranging from human resources to academics to athletics. It is, in short, the board that defines and monitors the general purpose and strategy of the institution.

The second purpose of the board is less noble but no less important: it is a fund-raising opportunity for the university. Wealthy people are often willing to give their money to worthy causes. The trick is to make sure they believe *your* cause is the most worthy of *their* causes. One way to do this is make them invested in the success and importance of an institution by giving them a role in supervising it—and in many cases, universities will invite wealthy donors to serve on their board of directors. Some nonprofit institutions say explicitly how much money you must donate before they will consider you for a position on the board. University boards are rarely so blatant. But generally speaking, members of the board are expected to support the institution financially. And often potential board members are selected (and vetted) as much for their personal wealth as for their understanding of higher education.

A university or college president is the person with overall responsibility for setting the course of the institution and monitoring its progress. In cooperation with the board, the president crafts a vision for the institution's future, working to win support for this vision among the various parts of the university. The president supervises the creation of a budget to bring to the board for approval. He or she recruits potential board members and serves as the public face of the university. Depending on the size of the university, the president may have some role in the day-to-day running of the school.

Budgets and Fund-Raising

All of these administrative tasks are critical. But a president who can't raise money won't be long for the job. It used to be that university committees preferred to hire faculty members (professors) as presidents. In recent years, however, that trend has shifted. Increasingly, successful presidential candidates come from development and strategic planning. This change reflects the evolving context in which universities function. In the late twentieth century, the costs of running universities grew rapidly at the same time that support from state and federal governments (important, even for private schools) remained static or decreased. The result was a consistent budget crunch and increasing pressure on presidents to raise money for long-term planning and infrastructure: adding buildings, funding new programs, and so on. While circumstances vary from school to school, it is broadly true that dealing with money occupies a disproportionate percentage of a university president's time.

Working with the president to raise money is the unit typically known as *advancement*. Their main function is to increase capital flow into the university. The nuances of that process will vary by institution. Some universities have strategic plans and campus master plans—a blueprint for what the campus will look like in five, ten, and even twenty-five years—approved by the board. Sometimes the president has a set of ideas in his or head that is shared on a need-to-know basis. But regardless of these particularities of process, every institution strives to develop a specific set of priorities around which to organize long-range fund-raising objectives. Fund-raisers then set out to raise money to support these priorities. Programs not labeled priorities often get little attention or support, either in the short or long term. After all, asking for money for every program leaves every program short on resources.

Accordingly, long-term fund-raising tends to happen in waves, usually called *campaigns*. Each of these campaigns is an intensive effort to raise money for a small, specific, set of big-ticket items: often new buildings or new programs. They generally last three to five years and often begin with a quiet phase, an effort to raise money before the campaign is publicly announced, so the president can claim from the start that the campaign has momentum and support. Campaigns typically involve the entire campus; potential donors often evaluate campus commitment to a project based on the percentage of staff and faculty who make donations. And, critically, these campaigns overshadow all other fund-raising efforts of the university. Though the university will not refuse donations to other causes, virtually all of the time and energy of those raising money will go to the current campaign.

Under the supervision of the president, universities are split into a variety of operating units: for example, academics, student support, human resources, and the business office. For the purposes of this game, you need to worry about only one of these: the athletic department.

University Athletics

The athletic department runs all aspects of intercollegiate athletics. At most universities, it has an extraordinary amount of autonomy. It usually has its own mission statement, its own website, its own publicity and marketing department and, crucially, its own budget. The person charged with overseeing the department typically holds the title of athletic director (AD). The AD generally reports directly to the president. But because of the importance of athletics to universities and their donors, the AD often functions virtually independently of the president.

At a basic level, there are essentially three separate sources of funding for athletics at universities. The first is operating revenue: the money made through ticket sales, television/radio rights, conference affiliation, advertising contracts, and licensing the name and logo of the university in general and of star athletes in particular.[32] The second is fund-raising. The athletic department often has its own array of fund-raising events and strategies, ranging from golf tournaments to "personal seat licenses."[33] The spectrum of donors who give to athletics overlaps with, but is not identical to, those donors who give to the other areas of the university. Finally, the athletic department usually gets a subsidy from the general budget of the university. This subsidy comes from tuition income, student fees, and other revenue sources in the main operating budget. This money is collected from all students, regardless of whether they "consume" athletics or even care if the university has a team. It is, therefore, a transfer from people who are not athletes and who may not even attend games to those who are or do.

Across the country, most big-time athletic departments operate at a loss.[34] That is, each year they spend more money than they bring in. If you strip out the subsidies and account for expenses like debt service obligations (the amount of money a department is obligated to spend each year to repay loans—often made to expand or build stadiums, practice facilities, and the like), only a very few athletic departments show a profit. And for colleges with designations lower than Division 1, it is even less likely that athletics earns money.[35]

Second, as we have seen, most universities in the United States are members of the NCAA. This organization sponsors championship tournaments (except for the highest level of college football), provides a place for university leaders to discuss issues about athletics and serves as an advocate for university athletics. Significantly, the NCAA also crafts and enforces the rules all its members agree to follow. Most people who follow sports think about this power in the context of recruiting. However, the regulations regarding scholarships are equally significant, particularly for the purposes of this game.

Scholarships serve as a kind of financial waiver, or coupon, to offset the costs of attending a university. Students who receive an athletic scholarship have some portion of their tuition, fees, and room and board waived. They get no cash, but rather they are able to attend school for a free or reduced rate.[36] In return for this discount, athletes are expected to play on athletic teams for a maximum of twenty hours a week.[37] Crucially, these scholarships are given to athletes on a year-by-year basis. Accordingly, if a freshman athlete does not play well or gets hurt, the university may decide not to offer them a scholarship for the following year. Similarly, if a coach is fired, the new coach may "pull" that student's scholarship at the end of the year to offer it instead to a recruit more suited to the style the new coach wants to play.

Most people think of scholarships using the model applied to basketball or football. In these sports, in the highest level of competition, every scholarship is a full scholarship (paying the total cost of tuition, fees, and room and board). The NCAA, which regulates how many scholarships member institutions may grant, allows football coaches to offer up to eighty-five recruits a full scholarship. Men's basketball coaches may offer thirteen, women's basketball coaches, fifteen. A small number of other sports provide athletes with full scholarships (women's gymnastics, for example).

But for most sports—and even for football programs outside of the highest level of competition—coaches are given a certain number of scholarships that can be subdivided. For example, a baseball coach may offer a student a full scholarship, half of a full scholarship, or even one quarter, so long as all the fractional scholarships add up to no more than the total allowed for the team. As you play *Changing the Game*, this point becomes important. Title IX regulates not simply the absolute number of athletes but the distribution of financial aid as well. Because football has so many full scholarships, its influence on the gender distribution of financial aid is disproportionately large. Thus football becomes even more important in determining Title IX compliance.[38]

Third, as you've read, universities have claimed for over a century that sports contribute to their academic mission. Even people far outside of the university community can recite the phrase that players are "student-athletes." And athletics at many universities are now labeled "co-curricular" rather than extracurricular in a bid to fold athletics into the broader mission of the university. One might be skeptical of these terms. After all, the NCAA coined the term *student-athlete* in an attempt to ward off charges that athletes were employees and thus deserved to be paid and to be eligible for workers' compensation. Nevertheless, campus leaders suggest (and often believe) that subsidies from the general fund to the athletic department are eminently reasonable. They propose that athletics and academics reinforce each other, rather than conflict. They maintain that athletics give students across the university a sense of community. And they argue that universities serve not just their current student body but its alumni as well as residents of the region around the university. This service may not be outlined precisely in the university's mission statement, but it is nevertheless real.

Finally, there is significant research testifying to the intangible contribution of athletics to the university. For example, these studies suggest that athletics drives potential students to consider attending the university and potential donors to contribute to the academic and administrative wings of the university, not just the athletic department. In other words, even if the athletic department runs a deficit, or if student-athletes fail to get a quality education, sports at universities might justify their existence by the claim that the visibility they provide is worth all of the costs.

The Role of Faculty

In most corporations, the relationship between employee and employer is straightforward: the corporation pays employees for work in exchange for the profits of their labor. But in theory, universities are different. Rather than faculty being employees hired by the owners of the university, the faculty form the university's beating heart. They hire administrators to run the institution so they can concentrate on their unique skill set—the expertise they have in a particular field, expressed through research and teaching. Collectively, then, the faculty *are* the university: together, they make the important decisions for the institution.[39]

In practice, most universities don't really work this way anymore. However, the underlying principle persists that the faculty are in control of the school's academic life. Thus faculty must typically approve the creation or elimination of new academic programs. Faculty often set the rules regarding requests for exceptions from academic policies. Faculty often demand to know more about the day-to-day workings of the university than presidents may want to tell them. Broadly speaking, faculty see themselves as partners with administrators, with the right to help make decisions about the school's direction. This concept is known as *shared governance.*

Over time, students have demanded that they, too, be included under a broader umbrella of shared governance. Universities began to consider such requests seriously in the 1960s. In the early twenty-first century, almost every university has a formal mechanism for hearing student desires and for offering students a space in which to make decisions. The amount of formal power students have is limited. But the cultural impulse to include students in decisions has been powerful, and presidents and boards are loath to appear insensitive to student opinion.

For this game, faculty and students shape university decisions more powerfully than you might expect. This is why the president will hold a listening session and faculty will speak (and expect people to care what they have to say). This is why the student government will hold its own listening session (and, again, expect people to respond to their decisions). Neither group has significant formal power over athletics, but they do have informal influence that extends far beyond what "customers" (the students) and "employees" (the faculty) would ordinarily have.

Faculty also have one additional privilege, that of tenure. This is the long-standing rule that, at a certain point in their employment at the university, the university will grant to faculty members the assumption that they will be employed at the school for the foreseeable future. By tying their futures to the university, tenure gives professors an incentive to engage in long-term efforts to strengthen the school. It is important to note that tenure is not automatic. Faculty must apply for tenure and meet a set of rigorous requirements. Nor does tenure mean a professor can't be fired. Tenure can be revoked for cause—in other words, if a professor isn't doing his or her job. But it does give faculty some freedom to speak out about issues about university policy and actions.

The precise way in which tenure is awarded varies by institution. In *Changing the Game*, the president must forward a tenure request to the board of directors, which then approves or rejects the request. This is fairly common among universities, especially those that are small or medium size.

* * *

All of this background on the inner workings of American universities is meant to help you play the game. It should serve as a resource for you as you try to navigate a world that may seem familiar—but in reality is quite complicated. Use it in a way that helps you the most.

 PART 3: THE GAME

MAJOR ISSUES FOR DEBATE AND LEARNING OBJECTIVES

What does it mean when we say society must treat people equally? If, in fact, society has discriminated against a group of people in the past, is it sufficient to eliminate the legal barriers to equality? Or should a society act positively to eliminate the effects of past discrimination? Are there times when "separate but equal" is actually okay? Is it legitimate to favor one group over another if the purpose is to offer a chance to people previously discriminated against? If so, how much?

Human history is, in part, the story of societies that treated groups of people differently. The particular identity of the groups changed, as did the nature and degree of discrimination. Occasionally, a society even offered its constituent groups something close to equal rights and burdens. But, with few exceptions, most societies have treated their citizens based on their membership in specific groups rather than as individuals.

We often think the modern West is one such exception to this pattern. After all, the philosophical grounding of the West, dating at least from Hobbes and Locke and perhaps earlier, rests on the individual. Yet most Western societies continued to divide their citizens into groups and to discriminate against members of some of these groups. Governments almost always structured this discrimination through legal prohibitions or restraints. Laws prevented the disadvantaged from voting; from pursuing an education; from serving in the military; and even from interacting with members of other races, ethnicities, or genders (preventing intermarriage, for instance). Critically, however, these laws were merely the formal expression of deeply held cultural stereotypes and assumptions, ones that underlay the laws but went far beyond them.

Not until the twentieth century did many of these societies gradually dismantle such discriminatory structures. This effort proceeded in fits and starts, went more quickly in some countries than in others, and involved significant political maneuvering and sacrifice. In most cases, opponents fought change bitterly. Still, reform continued throughout the century and throughout the Western world. Increasingly, societies tried to live up to their rhetoric, to treat everyone as an individual (and treating these individuals equally), regardless of color, religion, or gender.

The questions this raised, however, were neither simple nor straightforward. Some people simply rejected the claim that members of other groups deserved equal rights or fought desperately to retain the benefits discrimination had given them. But even for those with the best of intentions, equality raised troubling issues. Equal rights, it turned out, did not guarantee equal outcomes. In particular, attitudes and practices in the past continued to shape social, economic, and political opportunities in the present. As a simple example, people who had never learned to read had a difficult time taking advantage of their newly won right to a university education. Could past discrimination be remedied without contradicting the principles at the heart of recent reforms? If legal equality did not lead to equal outcomes, was it acceptable and/or necessary to treat people, again, as groups? Is it acceptable to discriminate against the formerly advantaged, at least temporarily, in order to create real equality?

Changing the Game uses Title IX and the debate over athletics at the college and university level to examine what equality means in a democratic society. It takes as its starting point the radical change the passage of Title IX seemed to promise. As you have read, high schools and universities had historically excluded women from athletics. To the extent that women's sports existed, they operated under a different administrative structure with a different vision. Title IX seemed both to promise and to require that women be offered vastly increased opportunities to participate in athletics. However, it left several critical issues unclear:

- Does gender equality require sameness? In other words, must women and men play using the same rules? Must women and men play on one integrated team or is separate but equal permissible in athletics? Must men's and women's sports be administered by a common organization? Most important, must the two share a common vision for the role of athletics in education?

- How do you measure equality? How do you gauge whether an institution is making sufficient progress at redressing inequality? What role should the government take in forcing institutions to change to ensure compliance?

- How do you measure the effects of past discrimination in producing modern-day preferences? It has become common for opponents of Title IX to suggest that fewer women than men want to play sports. Others argue that offering women opportunities to play will in itself increase the number of women who want to play. Must institutions equalize the number of male and female athletes? Or is it sufficient to match opportunities to participate with already existing interests?

- Finally, is it permissible to discriminate against current male athletes and teams in the interest of providing opportunities for women? Was such drastic action necessary, given the realities of sports at colleges and universities?

Title IX seemed a simple law based on a simple principle. Its very simplicity, though, left these questions unanswered. The result has been a decades-long struggle about how to implement it. Opponents have waged this struggle in the courts, on university campuses, and in the broader arena of public opinion. At one time or another, women and men, athletes and administrators, and federal employees and university officials have argued, often bitterly, over each of these questions. While the number of women athletes and the visibility of their teams and sports have skyrocketed, such debates continue today.

As you've read, this game is particularly focused on gender. However, the same debates and issues emerged in the aftermath of laws forbidding discrimination on the basis of race, religion, language, and disabilities. So, this game uses athletics as a lens through which to view broader social issues and tensions.

In addition to the questions about gender equity and inclusion and women's access to education and athletics, this game has another objective. In focusing on the role of athletics itself in education and American society, it asks students to consider what competitive athletics contributes to education, to what degree the values and goals of athletics mirror the goals of democratic society, and how the new media landscape of the late twentieth century shaped (and continues to shape) the way we think about sports. In that sense, it asks students to consider carefully what education is supposed to teach them.

While sports are enormously important in modern American culture, their prominence is not at all new. As you've read, athletics played a significant role in American culture and especially in higher education beginning in the late nineteenth century. Already, educators, coaches, and public intellectuals extolled the importance of athletics in shaping the moral character, and thus the social utility, of young men. And, as early as the 1920s, scandals plagued college sports and university presidents lamented football's power to distract students from their studies.[1] Nevertheless, throughout most of the twentieth century, while individual sports and leagues rose and fell in importance, athletics as a whole continued its gradual ascent in American culture.

The relationship between Americans and sports changed significantly in the last two decades of the century. While there were many reasons for this, the rise of ESPN and sports talk radio both exemplified and exacerbated this change. The influx of money and attention from national media hungry for ratings (and thus advertising dollars) reshaped existing conferences, created national rather than regional markets, fed aspirations for high-profile sports like basketball and football, and radically reshaped budgetary considerations on university campuses.[2]

Once again, we can look back to the 1975 Immaculata/Queens basketball game at Madison Square Garden on the cover of this book as an illustration. When sports media outlets saw an audience—and thus a revenue stream—for women's basketball, they created opportunities for exposure that catapulted the sport into the mainstream.

Accordingly, questions about the role of university athletics proliferated in the late 1900s. Some of these were economic and moral. Could the upward spiral of financial costs be sustained? Should student-athletes be compensated beyond the athletic scholarships currently granted? Are winning sports teams really the best way to market a college or university to politicians or prospective students? While important, these questions are largely beyond the scope of this Reacting game.

Some questions, however, derived from fundamental doubts about the value of athletics to the student athlete. Supporters of sports argued for a century that playing sports teaches character, leadership, self-discipline, and other valuable qualities. As a result, they were fundamentally educational in nature. Moreover, they tied students, town, and campus into a coherent community. This, they explained, is why sports should be a fundamental part of the university experience.

Already-existing doubts about the truth of these claims proliferated in the second half of the century. How can student-athletes really succeed in the classroom with the demands their sports made on their time and attention? Is creating this sense of community worth the cost? Most important, were the values taught by competitive athletics really the values society really wanted young people to learn?

After playing the game, you should

- Understand the historical context of the emergence of Title IX and how Title IX impacted college and university athletics.

- Be able to articulate major debates about gender equity in college and university athletics.

- Be able to discuss common positions and responses in civil rights debates as illustrated through the role of athletics.

- Understand the ways various constituencies have imagined and articulated the role and impact of athletics as part of a postsecondary education and how that has changed over time.

- Be able to explain the ways modern media shapes our view of the world. In particular, you should understand how the modern media landscape has shaped the role of athletics in college and university education.

RULES AND PROCEDURES

Objectives and Victory Conditions

In *Changing the Game*, students enter the world of Upper New England University (UNEU) amid two emerging and intersecting crisis points: first, the rising tide of scandal surrounding the commodification of athletics and student-athletes at universities around the country and second, and more urgently, the developing rumors of Title IX infractions at UNEU.

Winning the game requires players to persuade and compel the UNEU Board of Directors to follow their guidance in its response to these predicaments. Some players will have distinct preferences in both areas; others will be flexible in one and predetermined in the other.

Only the president may offer proposals to the Board of Directors. Only the Board will vote on the decision. However, many of you will be able to introduce or influence the proposals the president ultimately presents. And each of you will have the potential to influence the votes by the expenditure of Personal Influence Points (discussed later in this game book, p. 45).

The Board of Directors makes final decisions regarding the University. However, if a court rules that a university policy is illegal, the Board must change that policy in a way that meets the court's demands.

Whether you lose or win depends on the game's final outcome. Decisions will be made (and possibly changed) during the course of the game, but only the end result matters in determining victory.

While victory conditions for many players revolve around the policy proposal voted on by the Board of Directors, some players may have other objectives. These objectives may be in addition to their position on the policy proposal or they may replace it. Each individual role sheet lists the specific victory objectives for that role.

The Setting: What Do We Know About UNEU?

Upper New England University (UNEU) is a fictional composite of several American universities. For purposes of the game, players may assume the following (see. Appendix A for a summary):

- The University is a mid-size private liberal arts university located in New England. It is well known and respected in the region.

- The University has flourished in the past decades. It has an endowment and relatively generous donors. However, it exists primarily on tuition revenue. Accordingly, enrollment and retention (that is, students who remain enrolled from semester to semester) are critical factors in the financial stability of the University. Any president and administration will be judged at least on the ability to keep students coming to the University.

- UNEU is a mid-level university athletically. Its football and basketball teams compete in an important second-tier conference. During nonconference play they travel across the country to play larger, more important programs. Both have been consistently, if not spectacularly, successful, the kind of teams that go to a bowl game (or NCAA tournament) every three or four years. If T-shirt sales and attendance are any indication, the University's brand is significantly shaped by athletics.

- As with most universities, the Athletic Department struggles to break even. Most years it succeeds, but does so with significant help from boosters. This is true with football as well. In other words, the football team is not the moneymaker that subsidizes minor sports. It does, however, receive most of the directed giving from donors (money given by donors who specify that the money must be spent on a designated sport).

- The University has for many years invested in increasing opportunities for female athletes. However, the number of women playing sports has been consistently lower than the number of men. This is true despite the gradual increase in the percentage of the student body that is female. Indeed, the University has a female to male percentage that is typical of that across the country, about 55 percent female to 45 percent male. The same is true of scholarships. Men receive, in total, more scholarships and significantly more scholarship money than women. The disparity in money is partly due to a quirk in NCAA rules, which essentially results in all football scholarships being full, while other sports may divide their scholarships into parts. (As discussed earlier in the game book, a tennis coach, for example, may be given four scholarships to be divided among ten players, while the football coach gets eighty-five scholarships to be given to eighty-five players.) Even after accounting for this, female athletes still receive less money in total than males. But the disparity is significantly less than the raw data make it appear.

UNEU Athletic Department Mission Statement

The Athletic Department at UNEU enhances the mission of the University by providing student-athletes with the opportunity to pursue excellence in the classroom and on the playing field. By doing so, we will teach students the values of teamwork, diligence, and personal integrity. Moreover, by fielding teams that are consistently competitive at the regional level and occasionally at the national level, we will enrich the local and regional community of Upper New England.

In particular, we are committed to

1. Creating an environment in which excellence is expected and rewarded. Winning, in the broadest sense, is the result of such a culture and is valued accordingly.

2. Supporting the efforts of our athletes to excel academically.

3. Supporting the academic climate on campus by raising the University's profile among potential students and donors, supporting both the immediate and long-term budgetary needs of the University.

4. Operating with both institutional and personal integrity.

5. Recruiting, retaining, and supporting the development of athletes of high character.

Game Play

Changing the Game is played in a series of sessions, each staged at a separate location. Some sessions may last more than one class period.

- The first official Game Session is a listening session called by the faculty triggered by recent revelations regarding the NCAA violations involving nearby University of Massachusetts. It is held in a university auditorium and led by the professor of political science. Its stated purpose is to discuss the purpose of sports at UNEU in the light of the recent scandals. This session ordinarily lasts two class periods. It should end in a straw vote recommending (or not) that the University adopt a new mission statement for the Athletic Department (and, possibly, proposing a draft of such a statement).

- The second official Game Session is a listening session called by the Board of Directors in response to a threatened suit over Title IX violations. Several players will present formal comments on the proposal and perhaps suggest changes.

- During the third official Game Session, journalists lead radio talk shows. The number of radio talk shows included in your game will be determined by how many hosts (journalists) there are. Your GM will give you more information about this.

- Sometime between the third and fourth Game Session, if the role is present in your game, the Documentary Filmmaker will show the trailer for his or her in-progress film to the class. Your GM will announce how and when the trailer will be shown.

- The fourth official Game Session consists of two separate activities. The GM will announce whether these are held simultaneously or consecutively.

  - The first activity is a fund-raising gala held to announce the official beginning of a campaign to build a new STEM complex for the University.

    - This event is hosted by the president and attended by the Board of Directors and others invited by the president. You should assume boosters, local politicians, media members, and other significant figures will be invited. It is up to the president (and the GM) whether students will be invited.

    - Such a gala is a highly formal event. You should expect to dress in at least business casual and perhaps more formally. Your GM will give you complete instructions.

- The gala will end in an auction to determine the funding priorities for the University for the coming year (the auction is discussed in more detail later in the game book).

  ○ The second activity is a listening session called by the Student Government and led by its president. The session will take place in the Student Union. Several players will present formal comments on the proposal and perhaps suggest changes. At the end of the session, the Student Government should indicate (through a vote) its support or opposition of the University president's policy regarding Title IX and possibly propose a different alternative.

- The Fifth official Game Session is a meeting of the Board of Directors (including those players who have acquired proxy votes). The Board will meet to vote on proposals regarding the threatened Title IX lawsuit, the role of athletics at UNEU, and possibly the tenure application of the professor of biology. After this meeting is concluded, the Board of Directors will hold a press conference to announce the results of its votes to the media and university community.

Your GM may choose to alter the order of these sessions, to delete specific sessions, or to add others.

Other Locations for Action: The Bar, the Quad, and the Kiosk

Debate over university policies is not limited to formal sessions called by university authorities. Rather, it happens spontaneously, over lunch or coffee, in the gym or weight room, and in offices or classrooms. Moreover, in universities, as in many other political settings, reasoned debate is supplemented by informal connections and social capital. People who want support may get it through informal lobbying, calling in favors, or harnessing social networks. In *Changing the Game*, such informal lobbying and debate is centered in three specific locations.

The Bar. In *Changing the Game*, each Game Session begins with a happy hour at a popular bar located just off campus (the player who owns the bar will reveal its name before the game begins). The GM will announce how much time will be spent at the bar each day. Here there is no formal agenda (although there is a player in charge—the bartender—whose job is to make people feel at home and to facilitate discussion). No speeches are given. During this time, students will have an opportunity to earn Personal Influence Points (see p. 45).

The Quad. Students (especially) and other members of the university community often appropriate public spaces as locations of debate. In *Changing the Game*, this is represented by the quad, the green space at the center of campus. Students often take over this area for studying, eating lunch, or simply napping between classes. Here, faculty members stop students to remind them of assignments and students stop faculty to ask them if they've heard about the most recent administration initiative. Here, as well, insightful university officials will mingle with student leaders, taking the temperature of campus and "showing the flag" for the administration. More important, students have traditionally chosen this space to make speeches, hold rallies, hand out fliers, and generally make their opinions known. Finally, here townspeople can take a highly visible stand on issues that concern them.

In *Changing the Game*, most players may request the current Game Session be suspended and game play transported to the quad. To do so, players need simply to raise their hand and announce to the GM their desire to go to the quad. If the GM agrees (they almost always will), whatever is going on at the moment is halted and the class is moved to the quad. The player asking to go to the quad may then take whatever action they prefer (make speeches, hold a demonstration, etc.), limited by the following rules:

- No member of the university administration or members from outside the University or town (reporters, representatives of national organizations, etc.) may request moving to the quad. This right is limited to students, coaches, townspeople, athletes, and so on.

- The class can go to the quad only twice per class session. Each player may request moving to the quad only once per class session. Some roles require the player to take the game to the quad. This will be specified in the role sheet.

- Sessions at the quad last a maximum of ten minutes. The GM may end the session at the quad at any point. This will ordinarily happen if the GM feels time is not being used productively. Only the player requesting the suspension of ordinary play or someone approved by that player may make a formal speech. However, *anyone* may yell comments, hold signs, start chants, or otherwise make his or her feelings known.

- The quad is, by definition, an informal setting. Every player will start out gathered in a central location listening to the person who calls the session. However, players need not remain in that spot. They may move away, perhaps to hold private conversations, or simply to show a public indifference to the opinions being aired.

Kiosks. All universities have boards where people post signs, notices, and advertisements. Often, these boards are filled with advertisements for coming events or classes. But they can also serve as places to post manifestos, alerts, and protests. The GM will designate one part of the classroom as the kiosk for the game. Students may post whatever materials they like on this space. The posts will remain for the duration of the game. No one except the author may *remove* such items. But it is the nature of this means of communication that players may place items *over* an already posted contribution.

Demonstrations and Other Kinds of Protests

People who feel excluded from or ignored at formal sites of debate and discussion often resort to unauthorized demonstrations or other kinds of protest to make their feelings known. Demonstrations in *Changing the Game* play the same role. They allow players who feel they are being silenced or that their opinions are not being heard to have a voice. They are an extremely powerful way to convey opposition or disgust.

These demonstrations are often more emotional, more inclusive, and less routinized than other aspects of the game. That does not mean, however, they don't have their own grammar and traditional strategies and practices. Accordingly,

- Demonstrations are *not* simply another location for speech; rather, they employ and embody a **separate set of rhetorical strategies and methods**. Players planning demonstrations should consider the ways demonstrations are traditionally structured and follow these principles. Demonstrations are not the place to make long, rational (boring?) speeches—they are places to use call and response, to sign songs or perform chants, to wave signs and placards, or to wear specific colors of T-shirts, body art, and the like.

- Demonstrations may take place on the quad, at the entrance/exit from Game Sessions, or even *inside* Game Sessions.

- For demonstrations inside Game Sessions, players in charge of Game Sessions may instruct demonstrators to cease. If they do not, the leader may eject the demonstrators from the room. The GM then serves as a kind of campus police and has the authority to enforce the decision of the chair. Note, however, that campus communities often believe strongly in free speech. Limitations of this right perceived as unreasonable may backfire.

- Demonstrations held before or after the meeting itself may *not* be stopped by other players. For example, demonstrations in the hallways outside of the classroom or that break out after the official closing of the meeting—metaphorically speaking, as the representatives leave the building—may be held without consequence. The GM will determine how long such demonstrations may continue before returning to other game activities.

- Demonstrations in the quad may last as long as the quad session lasts. The GM may instruct the demonstrators to move farther away from the speaker's platform to allow debate to continue (with chants/complaints in the background).

Any time feelings run high there is a chance events will get out of control. Accordingly, demonstrations will be accompanied by a die roll by the GM. This die roll will be modified by the intentions of individual participants and by the events of the game so far. The GM is the only one who knows for sure what might happen, but any college student should be able to imagine possible outcomes of a campus protest gone bad.

This game begins in April 1996. E-mail became widely used on university campuses in the early part of that decade. But the Web first emerged in 1994 and took until the early twenty-first century to assume the shape it currently has. Cellphones were large, ungainly, and expensive (and certainly didn't have cameras). **This constrains what kinds of things you may do at/for demonstrations.** For the purposes of brevity, you may do what you would have been able to do in 1996. If you have questions, ask the GM *before* you act.

Personal Influence Points (PIPs)

Informal social networks, reputations, and positions of influence are often as or more important than intellectual arguments. They can gain you friends, or enemies. They can get you positions: jobs, seats on boards of directors, and the like. And they can get you money, for instance by calling on people who respect you to donate money to your favorite cause.

Changing the Game uses Personal Influence Points to bring this reality into the game. PIPs should be understood as an abstract measure of how much influence you possess. Sometimes that influence comes from who you are and what position you hold. Other times, it comes from actions you take in the game that would win you support.

In the game, you can get PIPS in two ways. First, some of you will possess a specific number of PIPs at the beginning of the game. These represent the power you possess, derived from the position you hold, the friends you have, or the wealth you've accrued. Your role sheet will indicate how many, if any, PIPs you possess. If your role sheet does *not* specifically mention how many PIPs you have, you can assume you do *not have any* at the beginning of the game.

Players may also earn PIPs through specific actions during the game. PIPs will be awarded for:

- Designing a University logo/color scheme that wins the approval of at least 50 percent of the players.

- Wearing clothing with the University logo or colors.

- Writing and singing the University fight song.

- Taking part in a demonstration.

- Organizing a demonstration that attracts at least 25 percent of the players in the game.

- Attending a demonstration or listening session dressed as the school mascot.

- Persuading at least 25 percent of the players in the game to sign a petition addressed to the Board.

- Publishing particularly persuasive flyers/messages on the kiosks.

- Placing an article/advertisement in the newspaper or radio station explaining or endorsing your perspective on the issues of the game.
  - This is *not* a formal paper and should not take that form. Rather, it's an opportunity for you to explore different rhetorical strategies: satire, advertisement, cartoons, etc. If the GM judges the article/advertisement sincere and effective, you will be awarded 1 PIP. You can do this multiple times for more PIPs.

In addition:

- The GM will award 1 or more PIPs to the person most effective at presenting his or her perspective during each session.

- The GM will award 1 or more PIPs for the person most active during sessions at the bar.

- The GM may award 1 or more PIPs for particularly well-reasoned and written papers.

Players may propose to the GM additional ways to earn PIPs. This must happen *before* the player actually does the proprosed activity. The GMs ruling on such proposals is final.

What Can You Use PIPs For: Proxy Votes and the Auction. PIPs function very much like money. The GM may keep track of the players' PIPs, but more likely, the GM will distribute cards that look like currency to players who have or earn PIPs. They are your responsibility; if you lose the cards, you lose the PIPs. If you are caught trying to counterfeit PIPs, you lose the game and may be subject to additional, out-of-game penalties for academic misconduct. PIPs may be sold or traded—for influence, for votes, for chances to speak, etc. Any PIPs left unused at the end of the game are wasted.

However, as you've no doubt already figured out, not everyone on a college campus is equal. Each person fits into the campus hierarchy in a different way and each has different rights, responsibilities, and spheres of influence. No one is completely powerless—even students have the ability to vote with their feet, by transferring to another university. But some kinds of power are more visible and more immediate than others.

Changing the Game reflects this by limiting the ways various players can use their PIPs. Players in **student** roles may use their PIPs to

- Support (or oppose) a player who wants to sue the University. There is no specific cost to this—rather, the more PIPs that are donated to support or oppose such a suit, the more or less likely it is that the suit will succeed. If PIPs are donated both to support and to oppose, you may assume that the side with the larger number of PIPs has a greater chance of success.

- Win the support of other students: 1 PIP buys you the support of 50 UNEU students (turn the PIP into the GM and tell them you're doing this). You can then use these students in any way that would be reasonable in real life. You can announce that these students have signed a petition—for instance, that 50 people have pledged to transfer to another university if your preferred policy is not put into place. Or you may simply announce at any time that these students have taken an action. For instance, you can announce that 50 students have filled out the paperwork at the registrar's office to transfer to another college or university at the end of the semester or that 50 students have joined in your sit-in in front of the president's office or that 50 students have staged a protest on the quad. The more students you control, the more meaningful such threats/actions become.

- Attempt to support a specific program at the University by winning the auction. This is a critical part of the game. While the rules are relatively simple, they are very specific. So pay attention.

Players in **nonstudent** roles (faculty, administrators, donors, etc.) may use their PIPs to

- Purchase a proxy vote on the University's Board of Directors (cost is 4 PIPs).

- Purchase the right to insert an advertisement in a newspaper or on the radio talk show (cost is 1 PIP). This advertisement may, with the agreement of the GM, serve to supplement or replace a writing assignment. It may also, depending on the quality of the advertisement, influence public opinion in ways that will shape the response to Board decisions. Thus a particularly effective advertisement will earn the support of 50 members of the surrounding community (town residents, alumni, etc.). Throughout the remainder of the game, the player may then announce that 50 members of this community are withdrawing their support from the University, are canceling their season tickets, or are taking another reasonable action to support the player's position.

- Support or oppose a player who wants to sue the University. There is no specific cost to this—rather, the more PIPs are donated to support or oppose such a suit, the more or less likely it is that the suit will succeed. If PIPs are donated both to support and to oppose, you may assume that the side with the larger number of PIPs has a greater chance of success.

- Attempt to support a specific program at the University. This is a critical part of the game. While the rules are relatively simple, they are very specific. Pay attention.

UNEU has a number of budgetary priorities. Most important from your perspective, the University is in the quiet phase of a fund-raising campaign to build a new STEM center. Any donations could be used to support this campaign. Alternatively, they could be used to fund new teams for women, to construct better athletic facilities, or to be stashed for a rainy day.

Just before the board meeting, the president of the university (or GM) will hold an auction to determine which program the Advancement Office will focus on in their fundraising campaign in the following year. The auction happens immediately before the board meeting. The auction is silent—in other words, players will submit their bid in a sealed envelope to the GM, who will open the envelopes and determine which person has made the highest bid. The PIPs used for this donation go to the GM and are now out of the game. REMEMBER—you may trade or give PIPs to other players. Since the auction goes to the highest bidder, not to the policy that receives the most bids, it is important to strategize carefully about how to win the auction.

The person who "bids" the most PIPs gets the right to decide which program the university will support. That person is granted two budget dollars (see below) to spend as they wish.

In sum:

- Any time *before* the auction, players may purchase a proxy seat on the Board for 4 PIPs.
- Any time during the game, players may purchase the right to publish an advertisement in the newspaper or radio show.
- At any time during the game, players may announce that they are donating PIPs to support one side or the other of a lawsuit.
- The player who wins the auction is awarded two budget dollars to spend as they wish.

The University Budget and How It Constrains Your Choices

Universities exist in an increasingly competitive environment, and recruiting and retaining students is getting harder and harder. The UNEU budget reflects this.

Accordingly, you have a great deal of flexibility on *non*financial decisions (changes in playing time, etc.). But, when it comes to money, you must obey the following guidelines:

- Cutting a team (other than football) yields **two** budget dollars. You can assume the athletes on these teams will be allowed to keep their scholarships until they graduate.

- Cutting funding for football significantly (reducing the number of scholarships *and* reducing nonessential expenses; you may not do one without the other) yields **one** budget dollar. Cutting football entirely yields **four** budget dollars.

- Winning the auction at the end of the gala yields **two** budget dollars.

- Adding a team costs **two** budget dollars.

- Building/renovating practice facilities and purchasing new uniforms costs **one** budget dollar.

- Fully funding the first phase of the building campaign costs **two** budget dollars.

The president and Board may not run a budget deficit. If they make decisions that would cause a budget deficit, they must compensate for this by raising tuition. You can assume that raising tuition 2½ percent will raise **two** budget dollars of revenue each year.

Voting. The Board of Directors votes to approve or reject any proposal for eliminating/adding teams or revising the budget. It *may* consider any proposal offered to it. The only proposals it *must* consider are those coming from the president or Board members. It may choose to amend proposals or merge them together. If the Board does not vote, the GM will interpret that the same as if the Board rejected all proposals brought to it.

Each representative possesses one vote. A vote passes if it receives more than 50 percent of the votes. In other words, if there are five representatives on the Board of Directors, three votes are necessary for a proposal to pass.

Many of the players may earn the right to cast proxy votes (members of the Board of Directors may not earn proxy votes).[3] These votes are acquired by spending 4 PIPs. You may go to the GM at any time and purchase proxy votes before the final board meeting. If you have enough PIPs, you may purchase more than one vote. The GM, at the beginning of the board meeting, will identify who is on the Board and how many votes they have.

Boosters. Every university relies on donors who give money to support university programs. This is especially true with athletics, where prominent boosters often exert enormous influence over university decisions.

In *Changing the Game*, boosters have a certain amount of money they may offer to the University. This money is represented in the game by PIPs. As a booster, you may try to use these PIPs to support specific programs. You may either make donations in real time, or pledge to make them at the end of the game. If you do so in real time, you must hand your PIPs to the GM and tell him or her what program they are intended to support.

In contrast, pledges are simply promises. You may keep them or break them. You may withdraw them if people act in ways you disapprove. You may threaten or promise to do this in return for specific promises from the Board or president or to respond to decisions with which they disagree.

Just before the board meeting, the GM will tabulate the number of PIPs donated to the University to support specific programs. Only the program receiving the most PIPs will be supported.

Reporters and Newspapers

Changing the Game incorporates representatives of various media outlets in order to replicate the spotlight local news stories can have before a national audience and the reverberations that a national audience can have on local issues. With the advent of the twenty-four-hour news cycle in the early 1980s and the proliferation of special-interest journalism, seemingly small news items can make national headlines, with national outlets shaping the stories from thousands of miles away.

In this game, journalists from both local and national outfits will be covering the events at UNEU. They will almost certainly have points of view, as all journalists do, but they are obliged to follow accepted rules of journalistic ethics: reporting events and reproducing quotes accurately and showing at least some attempt to report all sides of the story.

The journalists will produce newspapers or media programs that may play an important role in the game. These reporters will cover events, share news of similar controversies in other universities, and perhaps break stories about individual motivations and actions. These newspapers and media programs will be available at the bar to be read, heard, watched, and discussed.

Journalists will search actively for sources on the controversy. There will be no formal press conferences. However, *once* per day, journalists may call for an interruption in normal game play. At that point, the GM will instruct players to stop their current actions and shift the venue back to the bar. Here, reporters will be free to circulate and interview various players about their actions and decisions. This interruption will last no more than five minutes.

Journalists will likely interview students outside of class sessions. It is essential that students check their e-mail for interview requests or written questions. Players are obligated to answer any questions asked by journalists. The answers may be long or short, specific or vague, truthful or not, as the player desires.

BASIC OUTLINE OF THE GAME

Changing the Game can be played using a variety of schedules. Two likely options are listed here. Be sure to consult your Gamemaster (GM) if you are unsure which schedule applies to your class.

TABLE 1

Standard

CLASS SESSION	SCHEDULED ACTIVITY	STUDENT RESPONSIBILITY	SESSION LEADER
1	Introduction to Reacting and to the game Receive your role	Read pp. 3–65 of the game book	N/A
2	Introduction to the game (cont.)	Read pp. 66–110 of the game book	N/A
3	Introduction to the game (cont.), faction meetings, school spirit vote	Read pp. 111–158 of the game book	N/A
Start of class sessions 4–8	Happy hour	Mill around and talk with other players	Bartender
4	Game Session 1 Listening session hosted by Faculty Senate	Play game Papers or speeches for designated players	Professor of political science
5	Game Session 1 (cont.) Listening session hosted by Faculty Senate	Play game Papers or speeches for designated players	Professor of political science
6	Game Session 2 Listening session hosted by president or Board of Directors	Play game Papers or speeches for designated players	Chair of the Board of Directors or president of the University

CLASS SESSION	SCHEDULED ACTIVITY	STUDENT RESPONSIBILITY	SESSION LEADER
7	Game Session 3 Radio talk show	Play game Papers or speeches for designated players	Radio host
Between class sessions 7 and 8	Screening of the documentary trailer	View and respond to trailer	Documentary filmmaker
8	Game Session 4 1. Listening session hosted by Student Government 2. Fund-raising gala: auction to be held at end of the session	Play game Papers or speeches for designated players	President of the Student Government President of the University
9	Game Session 5 Board meeting and press conference	Play game Papers or speeches for designated players	President of Student Government
Between class sessions 9 and 10	Screening of completed documentary film	View and respond to documentary film	Documentary filmmaker
10	*To be determined*	Play game Papers or speeches for designated players	Chair of the Board of Directors or GM
11	Postmortem	Discuss results of game	N/A

TABLE 2

Compressed Version

CLASS SESSION	SCHEDULED ACTIVITY	STUDENT RESPONSIBILITY	SESSION LEADER
1	Introduction to Reacting and to the game Receive your role	Read pp. 3–65 of the game book	N/A
2	Introduction to the game (cont.)	Read pp. 66–110	N/A
3	Introduction to the game (cont.), faction meetings, school spirit vote	Read pp. 111–158 of the game book	N/A
Start of class sessions 4–6	Happy hour	Mill around and talk with other players	Bartender
4	Game Session 2* Listening session hosted by president or Board of Directors	Play game Papers or speeches for designated players	Chair of the Board of Directors or president of the University
5	Game Session 3: Radio talk show	Play game Papers or speeches for designated players	Radio host

CLASS SESSION	SCHEDULED ACTIVITY	STUDENT RESPONSIBILITY	SESSION LEADER
Between class sessions 5 and 6	Screening of the documentary trailer	View and respond to trailer	Documentary filmmaker
6	Game Session 4 1. Listening session hosted by Student Government 2. Fund-raising gala: auction to be held at end of the session	Play game Papers or speeches for designated players	President of the Student Government President of the University
7	Game Session 5 Board meeting and press conference	Play game Papers or speeches for designated players	President of Student Government
Between class sessions 7 and 8	Screening of completed documentary film	View and respond to documentary film	Documentary filmmaker
8	*To be determined*	Play game Papers or speeches for designated players	Chair of the Board of Directors or GM
9	Postmortem	Discuss results of game	N/A

TABLE 3

Long Class Version (Class Sessions 120 Minutes or Longer)

CLASS SESSION	SCHEDULED ACTIVITY	STUDENT RESPONSIBILITY	SESSION LEADER
1	Introduction to Reacting and to the game Receive your role	Read pp. 3–65 of the game book	N/A
2	Introduction to the game (cont.), faction meetings, school spirit vote	Read pp. 66–158 of the game book	N/A
Start of class sessions 3–5	Happy hour	Mill around and talk with other players	Bartender
3	Game Session 1* Listening session hosted by Faculty Senate	Play game Papers or speeches for designated players	Professor of political science
4	1. Game Session 2 Listening session hosted by president or Board of Directors 2. Game Session 3 Radio talk show	Play game Papers or speeches for designated players	Chair of the Board of Directors or president of the University Radio host
Between class sessions 4 and 5	Screening of the documentary trailer	View and respond to trailer	Documentary filmmaker

CLASS SESSION	SCHEDULED ACTIVITY	STUDENT RESPONSIBILITY	SESSION LEADER
5	Game Session 4 1. Listening session hosted by Student Government 2. Fund-raising gala: Auction to be held at end of the session 3. Game Session 5 Board meeting and press conference	Play game Papers/speeches for designated players	President of the Student Government President of the University President of the University or chair of the Board of Directors
Between class sessions 5 and 6	Screening of completed documentary film	View and respond to documentary film	Documentary filmmaker
6	*To be determined*	Play game Papers or speeches for designated players	Chair of Board of Directors or GM
7	Postmortem	Discuss results of game	N/A

*The numbering of Game Sessions in the compressed and long class versions match those of the standard version and the keys in your role sheet. However, the *class sessions* in which the Game Sessions occur depends on the version of the game you're playing. Make sure you examine the schedule carefully.

OUTLINE OF ASSIGNMENTS AND DUTIES

Grades for *Changing the Game* are divided into two categories. GMs may choose to change the way these grades are weighted or the specifics of these assignments.

Written Assignments

Each student will write a significant amount during the game. The GM will decide how much each assignment is worth, but often writing collectively amounts to two-thirds of the grade for the game. For most students, this will take the form of two short papers. The number and types of writing will differ for a few roles. Specific assignments and due dates are listed at the end of each role sheet. Papers should be posted at a time to be determined by the GM.

A number of roles have the special responsibility of leading individual sessions of the game. These responsibilities are identified and discussed in individual role sheets.

Class Participation

Class participation is essential to learning effectively from a Reacting game. Players are asked to participate in several ways. Several players will have the responsibility of leading sessions of the game (see the game versions for specific listings). Players will also make formal speeches at various points in the game. Much of this game, however, is centered on impromptu debate and discussion. The GM will evaluate all forms of participation in assigning the grade for this section of the game. In addition, many GMs will count participation *outside of the classroom* (discussion, deal making, lobbying, persuading, etc.) in determining the participation grade. Recognize that the GM cannot evaluate out-of-class work unless they know about it. It is wise to ask the GM before the game begins how they would like you to inform them about such activity.

Note: Voting is expected for roles that include that power. However, voting alone does not constitute participation.

Outside Research

Changing the Game is set in a fictional university. However, the issues at the heart of the game and the national context in which they are debated are very real. A deeper understanding of your own role, of the historical evolution of your ideas, and of the historical reactions to those ideas will play a significant role in your ability to navigate the issues of the game effectively. Students are encouraged to do outside reading to supplement their understanding of the material. **However, students may not refer to events or introduce information before they occurred or were received in real life.** Put differently, you may not quote an editorial or article or idea that was published *after* the fall of 1996. In many cases, the ideas in such an article will be consistent with arguments made *before* the game is set. In this case, you may be able to use the general arguments within an article. But you may never use factual information derived from such an article or use exact quotes from it. If you are unsure about a particular case, consult the GM before finishing the assignment.

COUNTERFACTUALS

There is one central counterfactual in *Changing the Game*: that the game is located at a composite, fictional university. Because UNEU is fictional, specific details of budgets, teams, and local context are also imagined. Every attempt, however, has been made to make these historically plausible based on universities and colleges involved in debates at this time.

 PART 4: FACTIONS AND INDEPENDENTS

Before game play begins, students will receive a role sheet containing background information on their character, victory conditions, advice on strategy, and details of writing and speaking assignments.

Students should not show their role sheet to another person. You may, as you choose, share specific information from that sheet orally. If another player shares such information with you, you may choose to trust the disclosure, to treat it with suspicion, or to dismiss it as disinformation or falsification. In the game, as in life, there is no formal penalty for lying. If someone offers to show you his or her role sheet, be cautious. You may assume the instructor has e-mailed that player a supplement or replacement and they are trying to mislead you. If you provide someone a copy of your role sheet, the instructor may choose to assign you a failing grade for the game or even the course.

Generally speaking, two informal groupings will likely emerge during the game. Players in each of these groups broadly agree on how to address questions of gender equality in athletics. These shared assumptions and preferences will generally lead them to respond similarly to ideas or proposals. In that sense, players may think of themselves as belonging to a faction of people who want the same thing. However, unlike other Reacting games, this is purely informal. Each player makes decisions, votes, and chooses what ideas to convey in a speech, *as an individual*. Moreover, the proposal to eliminate a specific men's athletic team will undoubtedly provoke much broader responses and feelings. Players who share positions on that specific proposal may or may not agree on its wider implications.

There are several kinds of roles in the game. Some may be duplicated. Many, however, will be individuals. These roles are as follows:

1. Student-athletes: Some will be members of the teams facing elimination. Others will play different sports and will have varying motivations based on their particular situation.

2. Students: Their motivations and victory conditions may vary based on their particular backgrounds.

3. Faculty members: They may be for or against the various proposals set forth. They may also have broader agendas involving the role of athletics on campus and the position of the University in the community. Do not assume, however, they are automatically anti-athletics.

4. Coaches: As with student-athletes, they will represent a variety of teams. They may or may not share common perspectives on the various proposals and may have other agendas.

5. Members of the Board of Directors: The Board has the power to vote a proposal up or down. Thus members of the Board of Directors hold significant power in the game. However, they also have broad responsibilities and constituencies that complicate their decisions. Some may have preexisting opinions or agendas, while others may be undecided.

6. Residents of the town in which the University is located: university towns often revolve around the school they host. To some extent, this derives from the many jobs provided by the university. Often the university also functions as a cultural center for townspeople and a significant locus of identity. Townspeople attend concerts, go to art exhibits and lectures, and wear university logos. Frequently, they identify themselves as fans of university teams. Universities rely on townspeople as well for rental housing for students, for hospitality toward students, for a comfortable living environment for faculty and staff, and especially for donations. Residents often feel they have a proprietary interest in decisions made by the university and will lobby hard to make these decisions fit their own interests and desires.

7. Media members: Cutting men's teams is a big story in the middle of the 1990s. Any such debate will draw reporters and on-air talent from a variety of publications and media outlets. Some of these reporters have preexisting opinions and preferences; others can be convinced by thoughtful arguments.

8. Additional individuals with important roles in the discussion: Some are members of the university administration. Some are influential donors to the University. Some may represent national organizations that want to make a point on the national stage. Some will have preexisting opinions and preferences; others can be convinced by thoughtful arguments.

The following is a list of individual roles. Depending on the size of your class, there may be additional roles not listed here.

Brett Neil, President of UNEU. PhD in psychology. Taught and served as faculty athletic representative at University of Illinois, dean at the Ohio State University, and provost of Marshall University before coming to UNEU.

Jon Brady, Athletic Director. Played basketball at West Virginia University and coached at UNEU before transitioning into athletic administration.

Nancy Dennis, Professor of Political Science. Faculty athletic representative and chair of Faculty Senate. Fixture on campus, respected by students, faculty, and administrators. Coached volleyball for several years and played basketball in college.

Lorenzo Allen, Assistant Professor of Biology. Started at UNEU after completing his graduate degree. Beginning his sixth year. Up for tenure this year.

Don Yates, Associate Professor of Criminal Justice. Worked in corrections, then earned a law degree before getting a PhD in criminal justice. Faculty adviser for the UNEU College Republicans.

Eddie Carlson, Captain of UNEU wrestling team. Member of the Student-Athlete Advisory Council. Entering his senior year.

Carlos Scott, member of UNEU men's swimming team. Junior.

Gary Goodman, member of UNEU men's volleyball team. Has three sisters who played high school sports.

Gene Ellis, linebacker on UNEU football team. Senior.

Alexis Carson, Captain of UNEU women's soccer team. Senior.

Harriet Wallace, member of UNEU women's basketball team. Junior. African American.

Grace Perez, member of UNEU women's softball team. Junior majoring in sports management.

Lyle Greene, Head Coach of UNEU football team. Long-time staff member at UNEU. Well-regarded nationally for running a successful program.

Albert (Al) Mack. UNEU alum. Made his wealth from stock options at a high-tech startup. Now a manager at a financial services firm on Wall Street.

Drew Gardner. UNEU alum. Played football in college. Now owns a chain of car washes and several other businesses, including a local bar off campus.

Stacy Boone, UNEU alum. Pediatric oncologist. Played soccer at UNEU.

Bill Fowler, Mayor of Newtown. Born in Newtown and lived there most of his life.

Hank Stanley, Head Coach of UNEU wrestling team. Believes firmly in the importance of sports for preparing athletes for career and life.

Don Sharp, Chair of UNEU Board of Directors. Supporter of the sciences at UNEU.

Maryanne Cobb, member of UNEU Board of Directors. Alum. Played basketball at UNEU.

George Gonzalez, member of UNEU Board of Directors. Graduate of University of Michigan. Earned a law degree from Dartmouth University.

Maria Hammond, member of UNEU Board of Directors. Alum. Graduated top of her class in medical school. Now a heart surgeon in Boston.

Johnnie Craig, member of UNEU Board of Directors. Alum. Played shooting guard on UNEU's only Sweet Sixteen basketball team. Now, a sports anchor at a Boston TV station.

Carrie Peterson, Coach of Women's Golf team. Longtime member of UNEU. Began as a member of the Department of Physical Education. Played an instrumental role in the AIAW.

Tara Dunn, student, President of the Student Government Association. Senior. Member of the SGA since she was a freshman. Has served on committees with the president of the University.

Neil Holloway, student. Sociology major. Plays intramural sports constantly.

Deanna Bowman, student. History major. Fascinated with politics.

Ray Gilbert, student. Political science major. Played basketball and football in high school.

Faith Snyder, student. Business major. Wrestled in high school.

Jaimie Webster, journalist, ESPN. Graduate of Syracuse University. Part of ESPN's investigative journalism division.

Steve Pena, *New York Times* journalist, host of a sports talk radio show on WFAN. Played baseball in college.

Elenora (Ellie) Garza, student. Communications major. Editor of the UNEU student newspaper.

Rodney Stanley, Documentary Filmmaker. Earlier documentaries covered the return of Vietnam veterans, the campaign to persuade companies to divest from South Africa, and the southern strategy of the Republican Party. Passionate sports fan.

Catherine Lee, staff member of National Women's Law Center. Lawyer. Taught law for a year at the Ohio State University before joining the NWLC.

Gayle Riley, staff member of Independent Women's Forum. Political science major at Brown University, now has a law degree.

PART 5: CORE TEXTS

U.S. CONGRESS

Title IX, 1972

Title IX itself is remarkably short. Passed in 1972 as part of the U.S. Education Amendments, it contains very little in terms of detail or guidance for implementation. What exactly does the law say? Does it specifically mandate equality? Does it specifically address athletics? How might it impact women's lives beyond athletics?

SOURCE: *Education Amendments Act of 1972, 20 U.S. Code §1681.*

*N*o person in the United States shall, on the basis of sex, be excluded from participation in, be denied the benefits of, or be subjected to discrimination under any education program or activity receiving Federal financial assistance.

OFFICE OF CIVIL RIGHTS

Clarification of Intercollegiate Athletics Policy Guidance: The Three-Part Test, 1996

In response to the public debate about Title IX, the Office of Civil Rights (OCR) issued the following clarification of previous policy interpretations. It lays out clearly, if at some length, the standards that it would use in evaluating programs. What do these criteria say? How, if any, do they revise previous standards? Do they represent a change in the way the office will evaluate athletic programs? If you were an athletic director, would you be able to work with these guidelines? Why or why not?

SOURCE: *Office of Civil Rights, U.S. Department of Education, January 16, 1996.*

*T*he Office for Civil Rights (OCR) enforces Title IX of the Education Amendments of 1972, 20 U.S.C. § 1681 *et seq.* (Title IX), which prohibits discrimination on the basis of sex in education programs and activities by recipients of federal funds. The regulation implementing Title IX, at 34 C.F.R. Part 106, effective July 21, 1975, contains specific provisions governing athletic programs, at 34 C.F.R. § 106.41, and the awarding of athletic scholarships, at 34 C.F.R. § 106.37(c). Further clarification of the Title IX regulatory requirements is provided by the Intercollegiate Athletics Policy Interpretation, issued December 11, 1979 (44 *Fed. Reg.* 71413 *et seq.* (1979)).[1]

The Title IX regulation provides that if an institution sponsors an athletic program it must provide equal athletic opportunities for members of both sexes. Among other factors, the regulation requires that an institution must effectively accommodate the athletic interests and abilities of students of both sexes to the extent necessary to provide equal athletic opportunity.

The 1979 Policy Interpretation provides that as part of this determination OCR will apply the following three-part test to assess whether an institution is providing nondiscriminatory participation opportunities for individuals of both sexes:

1. Whether intercollegiate level participation opportunities for male and female students are provided in numbers substantially proportionate to their respective enrollments; or

2. Where the members of one sex have been and are underrepresented among intercollegiate athletes, whether the institution can show a history and continuing practice of program expansion which is demonstrably responsive to the developing interests and abilities of the members of that sex; or

3. Where the members of one sex are underrepresented among intercollegiate athletes, and the institution cannot show a history and continuing practice of program expansion, as described above, whether it can be demonstrated that the interests and abilities of the members of that sex have been fully and effectively accommodated by the present program.

44 *Fed. Reg.* at 71418.

Thus, the three-part test furnishes an institution with three individual avenues to choose from when determining how it will provide individuals of each sex with nondiscriminatory opportunities to participate in intercollegiate athletics. If an institution has met any part of the three-part test, OCR will determine that the institution is meeting this requirement.

It is important to note that under the Policy Interpretation the requirement to provide nondiscriminatory participation opportunities is only one of many factors that OCR examines to determine if an institution is in compliance with the athletics provision of Title IX. OCR also considers the quality of competition offered to members of both sexes in order to determine whether an institution effectively accommodates the interests and abilities of its students.

---

1. *The Policy Interpretation is designed for intercollegiate athletics. However, its general principles, and those of this Clarification, often will apply to elementary and secondary interscholastic athletic programs, which are also covered by the regulation. See 44* Fed. Reg. *71413.*

In addition, when an "overall determination of compliance" is made by OCR, 44 *Fed. Reg.* 71417, 71418, OCR examines the institution's program as a whole. Thus OCR considers the effective accommodation of interests and abilities in conjunction with equivalence in the availability, quality and kinds of other athletic benefits and opportunities provided male and female athletes to determine whether an institution provides equal athletic opportunity as required by Title IX. These other benefits include coaching, equipment, practice and competitive facilities, recruitment, scheduling of games, and publicity, among others. An institution's failure to provide nondiscriminatory participation opportunities usually amounts to a denial of equal athletic opportunity because these opportunities provide access to all other athletic benefits, treatment, and services.

This Clarification provides specific factors that guide an analysis of each part of the three-part test. In addition, it provides examples to demonstrate, in concrete terms, how these factors will be considered. These examples are intended to be illustrative, and the conclusions drawn in each example are based solely on the facts included in the example.

THREE-PART TEST—PART ONE: ARE PARTICIPATION OPPORTUNITIES SUBSTANTIALLY PROPORTIONATE TO ENROLLMENT?

Under part one of the three-part test (part one), where an institution provides intercollegiate level athletic participation opportunities for male and female students in numbers substantially proportionate to their respective full-time undergraduate enrollments, OCR will find that the institution is providing nondiscriminatory participation opportunities for individuals of both sexes.

OCR's analysis begins with a determination of the number of participation opportunities afforded to male and female athletes in the intercollegiate athletic program. The Policy Interpretation defines participants as those athletes:

a. Who are receiving the institutionally-sponsored support normally provided to athletes competing at the institution involved, e.g., coaching, equipment, medical and training room services, on a regular basis during a sport's season; and

b. Who are participating in organized practice sessions and other team meetings and activities on a regular basis during a sport's season; and

c. Who are listed on the eligibility or squad lists maintained for each sport, or

d. Who, because of injury, cannot meet a, b, or c above but continue to receive financial aid on the basis of athletic ability.

44 *Fed. Reg.* at 71415.

OCR uses this definition of participant to determine the number of participation opportunities provided by an institution for purposes of the three-part test.

Under this definition, OCR considers a sport's season to commence on the date of a team's first intercollegiate competitive event and to conclude on the date of the team's final intercollegiate competitive event. As a general rule, all athletes who are listed on a team's squad or eligibility list and are on the team as of the team's first competitive event are counted as participants by OCR. In determining the number of participation opportunities for the purposes of the interests and abilities analysis, an athlete who participates in more than one sport will be counted as a participant in each sport in which he or she participates.

In determining participation opportunities, OCR includes, among others, those athletes who do not receive scholarships (e.g., walk-ons), those athletes who compete on teams sponsored by the institution even though the team may be required to raise some or all of its operating funds, and those athletes who practice but may not compete. OCR's investigations reveal that these athletes receive numerous benefits and services, such as training and practice time, coaching, tutoring services, locker room facilities, and equipment, as well as important non-tangible benefits derived from being a member of an intercollegiate athletic team. Because these are significant benefits, and because receipt of these benefits does not depend on their cost to the institution or whether the athlete competes, it is necessary to count all athletes who receive such benefits when determining the number of athletic opportunities provided to men and women.

OCR's analysis next determines whether athletic opportunities are substantially proportionate. The Title IX regulation allows institutions to operate separate athletic programs for men and women. Accordingly, the regulation allows an institution to control the respective number of participation opportunities offered to men and women. Thus, it could be argued that to satisfy part one there should be no difference between the participation rate in an institution's intercollegiate athletic program and its full-time undergraduate student enrollment.

However, because in some circumstances it may be unreasonable to expect an institution to achieve exact proportionality—for instance, because of natural fluctuations in enrollment and participation rates or because it would be unreasonable to expect an institution to add athletic opportunities in light of the small number of students that would have to be accommodated to achieve exact proportionality—the Policy Interpretation examines whether participation opportunities are "substantially" proportionate to enrollment rates. Because this determination depends on the institution's specific circumstances and the size of its athletic program, OCR makes this determination on a case-by-case basis, rather than through use of a statistical test.

As an example of a determination under part one: If an institution's enrollment is 52 percent male and 48 percent female and 52 percent of the participants in the athletic program are male and 48 percent female, then the institution would clearly satisfy part one. However, OCR recognizes that natural fluctuations in an institution's enrollment and/or participation rates may affect the percentages in a subsequent year. For instance, if the institution's admissions the following year resulted in an enrollment rate of 51 percent males and 49 percent females, while the participation rates of males and females in the athletic program remained constant, the institution would continue to satisfy part one because it would be unreasonable to expect the institution to fine tune its program in response to this change in enrollment.

As another example, over the past five years an institution has had a consistent enrollment rate for women of 50 percent. During this time period, it has been expanding its program for women in order to reach proportionality. In the year that the institution reaches its goal—i.e., 50 percent of the participants in its athletic program are female—its enrollment rate for women increases to 52 percent. Under these circumstances, the institution would satisfy part one.

OCR would also consider opportunities to be substantially proportionate when the number of opportunities that would be required to achieve proportionality would not be sufficient to sustain a viable team, i.e., a team for which there is a sufficient number of interested and able students and enough available competition to sustain an intercollegiate team. As a frame of reference in assessing this situation, OCR may consider the average size of teams offered for the underrepresented sex, a number which would vary by institution.

For instance, Institution A is a university with a total of 600 athletes. While women make up 52 percent of the university's enrollment, they only represent 47 percent of its athletes. If the university provided women with 52 percent of athletic opportunities, approximately 62 additional women would be able to participate. Because this is a significant number of unaccommodated women, it is likely that a viable sport could be added. If so, Institution A ha s not met part one.

As another example, at Institution B women also make up 52 percent of the university's enrollment and represent 47 percent of Institution B's athletes. Institution B's athletic program consists of only 60 participants. If the University provided women with 52 percent of athletic opportunities, approximately 6 additional women would be able to participate. Since 6 participants are unlikely to support a viable team, Institution B would meet part one.

THREE-PART TEST—PART TWO: IS THERE A HISTORY AND CONTINUING PRACTICE OF PROGRAM EXPANSION FOR THE UNDERREPRESENTED SEX?

Under part two of the three-part test (part two), an institution can show that it has a history and continuing practice of program expansion which is demonstrably responsive to the developing interests and abilities of the underrepresented sex. In effect, part two looks at an institution's past and continuing remedial efforts to provide nondiscriminatory participation opportunities through program expansion.[2]

OCR will review the entire history of the athletic program, focusing on the participation opportunities provided for the underrepresented sex. First, OCR will assess whether past actions of the institution have expanded participation opportunities for the underrepresented sex in a manner that was demonstrably responsive to their developing interests and abilities. Developing interests include interests that already exist at the institution.[3] There are no fixed intervals of time within which an institution must have added participation opportunities. Neither is a particular number of sports dispositive. Rather, the focus is on whether the program expansion was responsive to developing interests and abilities of the underrepresented sex. In addition, the institution must demonstrate a continuing (i.e., present) practice of program expansion as warranted by developing interests and abilities.

OCR will consider the following factors, among others, as evidence that may indicate a history of program expansion that is demonstrably responsive to the developing interests and abilities of the underrepresented sex:

- an institution's record of adding intercollegiate teams, or upgrading teams to intercollegiate status, for the underrepresented sex;

- an institution's record of increasing the numbers of participants in intercollegiate athletics who are members of the underrepresented sex; and

- an institution's affirmative responses to requests by students or others for addition or elevation of sports.

OCR will consider the following factors, among others, as evidence that may indicate a continuing practice of program expansion that is demonstrably responsive to the developing interests and abilities of the underrepresented sex:

- an institution's current implementation of a nondiscriminatory policy or procedure for requesting the addition of sports (including the eleva-

---

2. Part two focuses on whether an institution has expanded the number of intercollegiate participation opportunities provided to the underrepresented sex. Improvements in the quality of competition, and of other athletic benefits, provided to women athletes, while not considered under the three-part test, can be considered by OCR in making an overall determination of compliance with the athletics provision of Title IX.

3. However, under this part of the test an institution is not required, as it is under part three, to accommodate all interests and abilities of the underrepresented sex. Moreover, under part two an institution has flexibility in choosing which teams it adds for the underrepresented sex, as long as it can show overall a history and continuing practice of program expansion for members of that sex.

tion of club or intramural teams) and the effective communication of the policy or procedure to students; and

- an institution's current implementation of a plan of program expansion that is responsive to developing interests and abilities.

OCR would also find persuasive an institution's efforts to monitor developing interests and abilities of the underrepresented sex, for example, by conducting periodic nondiscriminatory assessments of developing interests and abilities and taking timely actions in response to the results.

In the event that an institution eliminated any team for the underrepresented sex, OCR would evaluate the circumstances surrounding this action in assessing whether the institution could satisfy part two of the test. However, OCR will not find a history and continuing practice of program expansion where an institution increases the proportional participation opportunities for the underrepresented sex by reducing opportunities for the overrepresented sex alone or by reducing participation opportunities for the overrepresented sex to a proportionately greater degree than for the underrepresented sex. This is because part two considers an institution's good faith remedial efforts through actual program expansion. It is only necessary to examine part two if one sex is overrepresented in the athletic program. Cuts in the program for the underrepresented sex, even when coupled with cuts in the program for the overrepresented sex, cannot be considered remedial because they burden members of the sex already disadvantaged by the present program. However, an institution that has eliminated some participation opportunities for the underrepresented sex can still meet part two if, overall, it can show a history and continuing practice of program expansion for that sex.

In addition, OCR will not find that an institution satisfies part two where it established teams for the underrepresented sex only at the initiation of its program for the underrepresented sex or where it merely promises to expand its program for the underrepresented sex at some time in the future.

The following examples are intended to illustrate the principles discussed above.

At the inception of its women's program in the mid-1970s, Institution C established seven teams for women. In 1984 it added a women's varsity team at the request of students and coaches. In 1990 it upgraded a women's club sport to varsity team status based on a request by the club members and an NCAA survey that showed a significant increase in girls high school participation in that sport. Institution C is currently implementing a plan to add a varsity women's team in the spring of 1996 that has been identified by a regional study as an emerging women's sport in the region. The addition of these teams resulted in an increased percentage of women participating in varsity athletics at the institution. Based on these facts, OCR would find Institution C in compliance with part two because it has a history of program expansion and is continuing to expand its program for women to meet their developing interests and abilities.

By 1980, Institution D established seven teams for women. Institution D added a women's varsity team in 1983 based on the requests of students and coaches. In 1991 it added a women's varsity team after an NCAA survey showed a significant increase in girls' high school participation in that sport. In 1993 Institution D eliminated a viable women's team and a viable men's team in an effort to reduce its athletic budget. It has taken no action relating to the underrepresented sex since 1993. Based on these facts, OCR would not find Institution D in compliance with part two. Institution D cannot show a continuing practice of program expansion that is responsive to the developing interests and abilities of the underrepresented sex where its only action since 1991 with regard to the underrepresented sex was to eliminate a team for which there was interest, ability and available competition.

In the mid-1970s, Institution E established five teams for women. In 1979 it added a women's varsity team. In 1984 it upgraded a women's club sport with twenty-five participants to varsity team status. At that time it eliminated a women's varsity team that had eight members. In 1987 and 1989 Institution E added women's varsity teams that were identified by a significant number of its enrolled and incoming female students when surveyed regarding their athletic interests and abilities. During this time it also increased the size of an existing women's team to provide opportunities for women who expressed interest in playing that sport. Within the past year, it added a women's varsity team based on a nationwide survey of the most popular girls high school teams. Based on the addition of these teams, the percentage of women participating in varsity athletics at the institution has increased. Based on these facts, OCR would find Institution E in compliance with part two because it has a history of program expansion and the elimination of the team in 1984 took place within the context of continuing program expansion for the underrepresented sex that is responsive to their developing interests.

Institution F started its women's program in the early 1970s with four teams. It did not add to its women's program until 1987 when, based on requests of students and coaches, it upgraded a women's club sport to varsity team status and expanded the size of several existing women's teams to accommodate significant expressed interest by students. In 1990 it surveyed its enrolled and incoming female students; based on that survey and a survey of the most popular sports played by women in the region, Institution F agreed to add three new women's teams by 1997. It added a women's team in 1991 and 1994. Institution F is implementing a plan to add a women's team by the spring of 1997. Based on these facts, OCR would find Institution F in compliance with part two. Institution F's program history since 1987 shows that it is committed to program expansion for the underrepresented sex and it is continuing to expand its women's program in light of women's developing interests and abilities.

THREE-PART TEST—PART THREE: IS THE INSTITUTION FULLY AND EFFECTIVELY ACCOMMODATING THE INTERESTS AND ABILITIES OF THE UNDERREPRESENTED SEX?

Under part three of the three-part test (part three) OCR determines whether an institution is fully and effectively accommodating the interests and abilities of its students who are members of the underrepresented sex—including students who are admitted to the institution though not yet enrolled. Title IX provides that at recipient must provide equal athletic opportunity to its students. Accordingly, the Policy Interpretation does not require an institution to accommodate the interests and abilities of potential students.[4]

While disproportionately high athletic participation rates by an institution's students of the overrepresented sex (as compared to their enrollment rates) may indicate that an institution is not providing equal athletic opportunities to its students of the underrepresented sex, an institution can satisfy part three where there is evidence that the imbalance does not reflect discrimination, i.e., where it can be demonstrated that, notwithstanding disproportionately low participation rates by the institution's students of the underrepresented sex, the interests and abilities of these students are, in fact, being fully and effectively accommodated.

In making this determination, OCR will consider whether there is (a) unmet interest in a particular sport; (b) sufficient ability to sustain a team in the sport; and (c) a reasonable expectation of competition for the team. If all three conditions are present OCR will find that an institution has not fully and effectively accommodated the interests and abilities of the underrepresented sex.

If an institution has recently eliminated a viable team from the intercollegiate program, OCR will find that there is sufficient interest, ability, and available competition to sustain an intercollegiate team in that sport unless an institution can provide strong evidence that interest, ability, or available competition no longer exists.

a) Is There Sufficient Unmet Interest to Support an Intercollegiate Team?

OCR will determine whether there is sufficient unmet interest among the institution's students who are members of the underrepresented sex to sustain an intercollegiate team. OCR will look for interest by the underrepresented sex as expressed through the following indicators, among others:

---

4. *However, OCR does examine an institution's recruitment practices under another part of the Policy Interpretation. See 44 Fed. Reg. 71417. Accordingly, where an institution recruits potential student athletes for its men's teams, it must ensure that women's teams are provided with substantially equal opportunities to recruit potential student athletes.*

- requests by students and admitted students that a particular sport be added;

- requests that an existing club sport be elevated to intercollegiate team status;

- participation in particular club or intramural sports;

- interviews with students, admitted students, coaches, administrators and others regarding interest in particular sports;

- results of questionnaires of students and admitted students regarding interests in particular sports; and

- participation in particular in interscholastic sports by admitted students.

In addition, OCR will look at participation rates in sports in high schools, amateur athletic associations, and community sports leagues that operate in areas from which the institution draws its students in order to ascertain likely interest and ability of its students and admitted students in particular sport(s).[5] For example, where OCR's investigation finds that a substantial number of high schools from the relevant region offer a particular sport which the institution does not offer for the underrepresented sex, OCR will ask the institution to provide a basis for any assertion that its students and admitted students are not interested in playing that sport. OCR may also interview students, admitted students, coaches, and others regarding interest in that sport.

An institution may evaluate its athletic program to assess the athletic interest of its students of the underrepresented sex using nondiscriminatory methods of its choosing. Accordingly, institutions have flexibility in choosing a nondiscriminatory method of determining athletic interests and abilities provided they meet certain requirements. See 44 *Fed. Reg.* at 71417. These assessments may use straightforward and inexpensive techniques, such as a student questionnaire or an open forum, to identify students' interests and abilities. Thus, while OCR expects that an institution's assessment should reach a wide audience of students and should be open-ended regarding the sports students can express interest in, OCR does not require elaborate scientific validation of assessments.

An institution's evaluation of interest should be done periodically so that the institution can identify in a timely and responsive manner any developing interests and abilities of the underrepresented sex. The evaluation should also take into account sports played in the high schools and communities from which the insti-

---

5. *While these indications of interest may be helpful to OCR in ascertaining likely interest on campus, particularly in the absence of more direct indicia, an institution is expected to meet the actual interests and abilities of its students and admitted students.*

tution draws its students both as an indication of possible interest on campus and to permit the institution to plan to meet the interests of admitted students of the underrepresented sex.

b) Is There Sufficient Ability to Sustain an Intercollegiate Team?

Second, OCR will determine whether there is sufficient ability among interested students of the underrepresented sex to sustain an intercollegiate team. OCR will examine indications of ability such as:

- the athletic experience and accomplishments—in interscholastic, club or intramural competition—of students and admitted students interested in playing the sport;

- opinions of coaches, administrators, and athletes at the institution regarding whether interested students and admitted students have the potential to sustain a varsity team; and

- if the team has previously competed at the club or intramural level, whether the competitive experience of the team indicates that it has the potential to sustain an intercollegiate team.

Neither a poor competitive record not the inability of interested students or admitted students to play at the same level of competition engaged in by the institution's other athletes is conclusive evidence of lack of ability. It is sufficient that interested students and admitted students have the potential to sustain an intercollegiate team.

c) Is There a Reasonable Expectation of Competition for the Team?

Finally, OCR determine whether there is a reasonable expectation of intercollegiate competition for a particular sport in the institution's normal competitive region. In evaluating available competition, OCR will look at available competitive opportunities in the geographic area in which the institution's athletes primarily compete, including:

- competitive opportunities offered by other schools against which the institution competes; and

- competitive opportunities offered by other schools in the institution's geographic area, including those offered by schools against which the institution does not now compete.

Under the Policy Interpretation, the institution may also be required to actively encourage the development of intercollegiate competition for a sport for members of the underrepresented sex when overall athletic opportunities within its competitive region have been historically limited for members of that sex.

CONCLUSION

This discussion clarifies that institutions have three distinct ways to provide individuals of each sex with nondiscriminatory participation opportunities. The three-part test gives institutions flexibility and control over their athletics programs. For instance, the test allows institutions to respond to different levels of interest by its male and female students. Moreover, nothing in the three-part test requires an institution to eliminate participation opportunities for men.

At the same time, this flexibility must be used by institutions consistent with Title IX's requirement that they not discriminate on the basis of sex. OCR recognizes that institutions face challenges in providing nondiscriminatory participation opportunities for their students and will continue to assist institutions in finding ways to meet these challenges.

ALL-AMERICAN GIRLS PROFESSIONAL BASEBALL LEAGUE

Rules of Conduct, 1943–1954

The All-American Girls Professional Baseball League (one of several names for the league) was formed in 1945 as a way to keep American attention on baseball while many Major League (male) players were serving in the military during World War II. It was a modest success at the time, lasting until 1954 and drawing over 900,000 fans in 1948.

The league recognized the challenge in drawing fans to watch women play baseball. In particular, league officials were acutely aware of the need to convince potential ticket buyers that sports did not make women less feminine (or turn women into lesbians). Accordingly, it went to great lengths to manage its players' lives to make them match traditional expectations of feminine appearance and behavior. What limits and expectations do the rules of conduct set for women? What do these tell us about how women were expected to behave and look in the 1940s?

SOURCE: *All-American Girls Professional Baseball League. Accessed at http://www.aagpbl.org/history /rules-of-conduct.*

*T*he management sets a high standard for the girls selected for the different clubs and expects them to live up to the code of conduct which recognizes that standard. There are general regulations necessary as a means of maintaining order and organizing clubs into a working procedure.

1. ALWAYS appear in feminine attire when not actively engaged in practice or playing ball. This regulation continues through the playoffs for all, even though your team is not participating. AT NO TIME MAY A PLAYER APPEAR IN THE STANDS IN THIER UNIFORM, OR WEAR SLACKS OR SHORTS IN PUBLIC.

2. Boyish bobs are not permissible and in general your hair should be well groomed at all times with longer hair preferable to short hair cuts. Lipstick should always be on.

3. Smoking or drinking is not permissible in public places. Liquor drinking will not be permissible under any circumstances. Other intoxicating drinks in limited portions with after-game meal only, will be allowed. Obscene language will not be allowed at any time.

4. All social engagements must be approved by chaperone. Legitimate requests for dates can be allowed by chaperones.

5. Jewelry must not be worn during game or practice, regardless of type.

6. All living quarters and eating places must be approved by the chaperones. No player shall change her residence without the permission of the chaperone.

7. For emergency purposes, it is necessary that you leave notice of your whereabouts and your home phone.

8. Each club will establish a satisfactory place to eat, and a time when all members must be in their individual rooms. In general, the lapse of time will be two hours after the finish of the last game, but in no case later than 12:30 a.m. Players must respect hotel regulations as to other guests after this hour, maintaining conduct in accordance with high standards set by the league.

9. Always carry your employee's pass as a means of identification for entering the various parks. This pass is NOT transferable.

10. Relatives, friends, and visitors are not allowed on the bench at anytime.

11. Due to shortage of equipment, baseballs must not be given as souvenirs without permission from the Management.

12. Baseball uniform skirts shall not be shorter than six inches above the knee—cap.

13. In order to sustain the complete spirit of rivalry between clubs, the members of different clubs must not fraternize at any time during season. After the opening day of the season, fraternizing will be subject to heavy penalties. This also means in particular: room parties, auto trips to out of the way eating places, etc. However, friendly discussions in lobbies with opposing players are permissible. Players should never approach the opposing manager or chaperone about being transferred.

14. When traveling, the members of the clubs must be at the station thirty minutes before departure time. Anyone missing arranged transportation will have to pay her own fare.

15. Players will not be allowed to drive their cars past their city's limits without the special permission of their manager. Each team will travel as a unit via method of travel provided for the league.

Fines of five dollars for first offense, ten dollars for second, and suspension for third, will automatically be imposed for breaking any of the above rules.

HEATHER ROSS MILLER

Half-Court Basketball: Power and Sex, 1992

Unlike many of the writers reprinted here, Heather Ross Miller is relatively unknown (she is a novelist who has published several books).

To what degree were women's sports treated as second class in the 1950s? Why? Did Miller realize that at the time? Looking back on the period, what does Miller regret? What does she treasure?

SOURCE: Witness Magazine 6, no. 2 (1992): 42–49.

*I*t took romance.

That old half-court ball we played in the '50s.

A blinding goofy romance flared every Tuesday and Friday night in the freckled gleam of long legs and white sneakers squeaking off the bright waxed floor of the Badin High School gymnasium. Our teenage breasts brushed against the ball before we slung it hard down the court to the tall forward who drove to sink the basket and run up the score for the 1957 Badin High Watts, the Aluminum City Kids, our magic kilowatts sparking every move. Such magnificent girls thundering to the center line.

You slung that ball hard and grinned and didn't care who got in the way.

Two! Four! Six! Eight!

The cheerleaders like dervishes in saddle oxfords and red skirts sweated through their heavy black turtleneck sweaters stitched with a big red B.

Who do we appreciate?

They didn't appreciate you. You were nothing but a guard. It was the tall forward they cheered. She got it all, you understood, that was the game. And but for the one hateful rule restricting girls to half-court play in 1957, keeping forwards and guards on the same team, six girls segregated into opposite ends of the hardwood, but for that one rule, you could have covered every polished inch of the floor, grabbing and passing and storming the opposition. Shooting baskets every bit as good as the forward. Mitzi Jane Blalock was her name.

What stopped you going the full length of the court?

Why didn't you?

Why didn't she?

We didn't know it was a sexual metaphor in 1957. We played that old half-court ball with vengeance and passion, like Amazons, like Valkyries, thundering to the center line. Then a dead hard stop at the center line, our ankles stinging from the concussion, and we slung the ball hard to one of the three forwards hovering there like bees at the comb. Mitzi Jane Blalock, the tall one, took it on to score, allowed only one bounce of the clumsy ball, no dribbling.

That's the way girls had to play until 1971 when five-on-five was allowed the full length of the court. But in our old game, three guards and three forwards circled in strict zones, a condition of cunningly segregated orbits. No dribbling. One bounce then pass. A dead stop at the center line. We thought it was the way you played girls' basketball. And playing was the thing.

And after the game, showered, pleasantly tired from winning this game of restrictions, we stretched on our beds and conjured up prizes for ourselves. Rich, good-looking men. Blue swimming pools. Strapless black evening dresses with thousands of sequins on the front.

Evening dresses! This old-fashioned garment is gone now. Now our daughters wear slinky gowns made of clinging stuff with spaghetti straps and plunging necklines down the *back*, their fashion sense sharp and demanding as Barbie's. In 1957, you were Scarlett, not Barbie. You played half-court basketball and wore evening dresses to dances, not proms. Always full-skirted, net and taffeta gathered to a tight strapless bodice, sometimes touching the floor, sometimes your ankles.

In the ninth grade, these garments were yellow stuff, ankle-length, strapless, with a little scrap of yellow stuff to throw around your shoulders, a stole you called it. Gold evening sandals with a slight French heel, the toes open, your toenails painted shocking pink. Carnations pinned to the bodice. Gold mesh evening bag with tiny hand-chain. And underneath these concoctions, a merry widow, a strapless item boned to the waist, pushed up your breasts, you hoped, toward a luscious cleavage.

Another blinding and goofy romance.

And gone for good like the half-court ball. The Howdy Doody days, the days of Fonz and The Three Bells singing "Jimmy Brown." A cozy American insularity. When basketball, not football, was the special pride of high school communities. And high schools were small two-story brick buildings still in communities, not big county conglomerates.

I'm stuck in my stereotypes here, lost in my nostalgia. How easy it is to make comparisons, to lament about the old days. Those good old days which probably are another kind of metaphor, another kind of hemmed-in half-court ball, sounding smug and coy, drowning in segregations.

I recently mentioned the old half-court ball to a good friend, an educated and sophisticated gentleman, and he said, "But it was so nice, the way you girls played back then. So graceful and feminine. Why do you want to go make something out of it?"

The way he said that brought back my old anger at the goofy blinding and romantic way we obeyed such expectations in those days. Half-court basketball for women in the '50s was the same as racial segregation: separate but equal. Except in the case of basketball, we were not equal. Keeping women on the half court was a definite form of discrimination. They said we could play ball but not the way *they* played it. We had a silly little game that really didn't count. Half court. Halfway.

In 1954, in *Brown v. Board of Education of Topeka*, the Supreme Court held segregation unconstitutional and called for change "with all deliberate speed." This had nothing to do with segregation by gender, including rules for basketball. So equality did not reach to the half court in Badin High School or anywhere else for another seventeen years.

And keeping women on the half court was the same as keeping blacks in the back of the bus, keeping separate but equal water fountains, keeping lunch counters pure white.

High school basketball was a peculiar situation, trivial perhaps, but nevertheless peculiar. World War II brought promises and opportunities to women, that splendid carrot of equality: the workplace. Rosie the Riveter in her khaki jumpsuit, permed curls teasing over her kerchief knot, may not have been dainty and charming, but she was indeed equal.

And surely she would be allowed to continue into the fantastic '50s, enjoying all the benefits of that wartime equality. This was not to be the case. The '50s disenfranchised women again. The war should have changed things for good, but didn't. For isn't it obvious?—if you can rivet together a war plane, you can run up and down a basketball court.

Instead, a few miles up Highway 51 from Badin High School, Catawba College let one outstanding woman physical education major play with the Bobcats for a while because the war had depleted the bench. She ran the full length of the court, drove hard for the shot, and held her own with the sweating guys out there. She also got her picture in the local papers as the *Bobkitten!*

The feeling was one of generous amusement, you went to see the *Bobkitten* play because she was a girl playing with all those guys. Not because she was good with a basketball. The Bobcats were amused, absolutely carried away by their own generosity every time she entered the game. The fans roared and applauded and pointed their fingers, "Lookathere, the *Bobkitten!*"

Such subtle segregation in sports continued. After a world war, after a Supreme Court decision. And the game became one of power, not sport. Because when you set women against each other on a half court, you don't have one team set against another. You have teams within teams, factions, hatreds, territories. Forwards and guards despised each other, a feeling that rose beyond the emblems and colors of the uniforms and settled somewhere in the realm of survival of the fittest.

So you had four teams out there on that polished hardwood, two on either side of that holy center line over which *they shalt not cross.* Every girl struggling to be another Bobkitten, wanting to show herself as the best, the feistiest, the one who could drive just like a boy if she had to, the one who, if a war came, could play ball with the best.

And why did they do that to us?

And why did we let them?

I'm amazed at how little I actually know anymore about basketball. I don't know who it was, man or woman, who forced the issue of the half-court restrictions in women's basketball. Or who got the rules changed so we could run the full length of the court, five-on-five, the way men do. Was it Title III? Was it *Brown v. Topeka?*

The official pamphlet of the Basketball Hall of Fame in Springfield, Massachusetts features the original Springfield College teams, those handsome lads with their quaint handlebar moustaches. No information is shared concerning the rules for women's basketball. Little mention of women at all, except to chuckle on page seven that when Smith College played, the gym was closed to male spectators because the girls wore bloomers. The chuckle continues, "Regardless of what the encounter revealed or didn't reveal, this indicates the sweet young things were as quick to appreciate the merits of the game as were the more stalwart members of the opposite sex."

Ever since I left those red-brick gymnasiums of the '50s, I've never had a single concern about the old half-court handicaps they forced us to play. The old segregation and the way we obeyed it.

Except to make jokes.

Because what did they think would happen to the *sweet young things* if we ran the full length of the court? That we'd get our periods? Or give birth to little babies right out there on the court, in front of our mamas and daddies and boyfriends?

Of course, women were thought to be weaker. And although the pain of childbirth is said to be one of the highest levels of pain ever recorded, we still couldn't cross the center line on the basketball court.

Or was it a last hedge against what was coming—the feminism of the '80s and '90s—which, of course, nobody could predict in 1957, least of all we girls playing out there under the cage lights in our lightning-bolt suits?

Politics, power, maybe even money lay behind the sexual segregation we accepted. I remember the dizzying classifications our schools had, Double A, Triple A, Class A, too dizzying for clear explanations. These classifications had something to do with size and location, rural or city. Whatever the motive behind the system, all rural or small schools had girls' basketball. Quite often city or bigger schools did not. But every school had men's basketball. And here's where it gets very peculiar. The bigger the school, the higher the classification, the more likely the school was not to have girls' basketball. This was never satisfactorily explained. More money and size ought to accommodate more teams.

And somewhere lurked a dark theory that when it came statewide tournament time, it wasn't seemly for the higher classification schools to compete with lower schools, especially when it came to putting girls out there on the court. It was okay for lower classification schools to put their girls on the court, but certainly not in competition with girls from bigger or so-called better schools.

So the game became not only sexist, but also elitist.

All the money, no doubt, went into men's basketball and their big statewide tournaments. Girls might compete at county levels, maybe even at small regional tournaments. But beyond that, not at all. The center-line rule was in effect in more places than the gym.

They never made any excuses to us about any of this or allowed any discussion. If you played girls' basketball, you stopped at the center line, got one bounce, and no dribbling. That was the way. You competed at certain lower classification levels. Your trophies came from the same hardware store as the men's trophies, but didn't really count. So it went. The happy blind obedient '50s.

And following the games, when we conjured up those fantasies I mentioned, the rich, good-looking men, the swimming pools, and the black evening dresses, we never conjured up lawsuits or test cases. We stayed on the half court and never crossed over. But I couldn't help thinking, what if, just once.

I used to fantasize driving around in a Thunderbird all over the small town of Badin, North Carolina, a white Thunderbird with portholes, like something the Bobkitten (wearing satin) might drive. I would pick up the two best-looking boys in Badin High School, Billy Trace who had exotic crossed eyes and Billy Rufty who had a five-inch scar down one cheek. They would peep in the portholes at me, then open the doors and say, Yes, sweet, anything you want, precious. And then they'd light my cigarette and hold their hands for the ashes and I'd say, Kiss my foot, and they'd say, We'll kiss any part of you, precious.

This was in Badin, an obscure and pleasant North Carolina town where nothing exotic ever took place beyond the smelting of aluminum, the aluminum that appeared in piles of bright ingots inside the smelter yard and then disappeared into the boxcars of Maryland-Pacific, Chesapeake-Ohio, Great Northern, Winston-Salem Southbound, gone in one night.

I was proud of my fantasies. I knew I wanted to get beyond the ingot yard, beyond the half-court segregation of the game I played so furiously. I didn't care much about Billy Trace or Billy Rufty with their crossed eyes and five-inch scars, except if I had to use them to crash the limits of my existence, I would.

I wish now I'd been clever enough to use the half-court basketball to take me places. Me and Mitzi Jane Blalock and all our other teammates in that peculiarly old-fashioned yet flashy Badin High Watts uniform: satiny black bloomer-shorts and a red knit tank top worn over a plain white T-shirt, the lightning-bolt emblem jagged between our breasts. The tank top fastened to little buttons concealed in the elastic waistband of the black bloomer-shorts. The other girls of the county teams wore more predictable uniforms resembling those of the men players: plain shirts tucked inside plain shorts. Or plain tank tops worn loose over plain shorts.

But the Badin High Watts were different. As the cheerleaders and the crowds assured us, not just our flashy uniforms, but our team effort, our origin, we were the Aluminum City Kids, you bet. Any girl who crossed this center line was doubtless doomed.

And all the time we went to school, all the afternoons we practiced in the big red-brick gymnasium, we heard, strong and rude as thunder, the booming of the Carolina Aluminum smelter at the edge of the town, Badin's never-sleeping industry, Badin's angry, overworked giant heaving away in the dark and the cold. Sparks showered from the crucibles and little flames clawed along the ingots as men sweated and aged. Everybody's father worked in the smelter in some capacity, carbon kiln, potroom, main office, rotary station, keeping the smelter going, turning out aluminum famous for its purity. Any man who crossed this center line was likewise doomed.

I meant to get free of such a place, such a game. My fantasies put me to sleep after each game won for the Badin High Watts. The smelter sprawled along Highway 740 and cooked furiously all night, devouring minerals, boiling up metal, and driving off the dross to produce silvery-white ingots we called pigs.

And all night I dreamed furiously about grabbing basketballs and slinging them down the court, hard, over the center line straight to Mitzi Jane Blalock. And then at some perfect moment in my dream, Mitzi Jane Blalock and I decided to run over the center line together, knock down the referees in their striped shirts, their whistles stuck in their mouths, and keep on running out of the gymnasium, downtown, past the aluminum smelter, and on up Highway 740, to the world, *the Bobkittens escape!*

We could have made it a circus ring, with snarling beasts and black whips and spotlights hot as sunshine beating down on Myrtle Beach. Men, emptying from the smelter potrooms, heading straight for the washhouse and the showers, would applaud our audacity. I'd tell them, Look at this, we are Venus di Milo twins in basketball uniforms, little stars twinkling in our teeth, stuck on our eyelashes, a hot burning light spilling out of both corners of our mouths. You never poured out any aluminum to match us.

But such daring, such a display, never happened. We played the game, anxious and swift, stopping like magic at the center line while the cheerleaders yay-yayed and rah-rahed us. We obeyed the zone. Stayed put. We couldn't tell what other maneuvers, other victories might wait on the other side of the center line—if we just broke through, just once. What futuristic ball courts dazzling with rich men and swimming pools, what black evening dresses with sequins might be our reward.

And maybe it's not even important in the history of American sports who first crossed over that center line in women's basketball, who broke the segregation of the old half-court ball. And maybe there's nothing to be made of the fact that Oklahoma and Iowa, those wholesome American heartland states, were the last to switch. There are no big deals in women's team sports. And except for the colorful stars in tennis or golf, the Olympic skaters and gymnasts, occasionally a swimmer or a runner—nobody really pays attention. Martina Navratilova and Chrissie Evert, Dorothy Hammill and Mary Jo Retton can get on a Wheaties box. And Florence Griffith Joyner can run in lace tights at the 1988 Olympics, an outfit almost as zany as our black satin and red lightning bolts of 1957. These women could wear merry widows and yellow net if they wanted. The old segregation is gone, that old half court, thank God, is dead.

In any case, to whomever she was who crossed first, I'd like to say I'm late with this—but I wanted to do it, too. My wind is gone now, my ankles and knees shot to hell, and my lower back crumbling into arthritis. But what I'd give to break across that center line, just once.

Running all the way in black satin, in lace, in sequins and lightning bolts.

BETTY FRIEDAN

National Organization for Women's Statement of Purpose, 1966

The National Organization for Women was founded in 1966 in the middle of a renewed movement for equality for women. It represented the emergence (already in progress for a decade) of a set of organizations and spokespeople who advocated for a new set of issues and policies regarding women.

Feminists (the term itself was and remains controversial, with different meaning to different people) in the later nineteenth and early twentieth century were primarily concerned with legal opportunities. They focused on getting the legal right to vote, on being admitted to colleges and professions, and so on. They won most of these fights in the early 1900s. However, it quickly became apparent that merely having legal access to the arena didn't guarantee equal treatment once you were there. Moreover, many of the concerns raised by women grew out of cultural and social concerns rather than legal ones. Accordingly, a new wave of feminists in the mid-twentieth century turned attention and efforts to these new questions.

The "Statement of Purpose for the National Organization of Women" offers a lens into this emerging effort. Written by Betty Friedan, it takes for granted the existence of many (although not all) kinds of legal equality. But it goes on to identify new issues that the new organization would take up and new understandings of rights that the organization would insist on. The statement of purpose doesn't address sports at all, at least explicitly. But it articulates a world view that would shape women's (and some men's) approach to sports and education.

What does Friedan identify as the goals of the organization? How does she understand "true equality"? How will you know when women have gained this? Why, according to Friedan, was it so urgent that women act "now" (in 1966)?

SOURCE: *Betty Friedan, National Organization for Women. Accessed at http://now.org/about/history /statement-of-purpose/.*

We, men and women who hereby constitute ourselves as the National Organization for Women, believe that the time has come for a new movement toward true equality for all women in America, and toward a fully equal partnership of the sexes, as part of the world-wide revolution of human rights now taking place within and beyond our national borders.

The purpose of NOW is to take action to bring women into full participation in the mainstream of American society now, exercising all the privileges and responsibilities thereof in truly equal partnership with men.

We believe the time has come to move beyond the abstract argument, discussion and symposia over the status and special nature of women which has raged in America in recent years; the time has come to confront, with concrete action, the conditions that now prevent women from enjoying the equality of opportunity and freedom of choice which is their right, as individual Americans, and as human beings.

NOW is dedicated to the proposition that women, first and foremost, are human beings, who, like all other people in our society, must have the chance to develop their fullest human potential. We believe that women can achieve such equality only by accepting to the full the challenges and responsibilities they share with all other people in our society, as part of the decision-making mainstream of American political, economic and social life.

We organize to initiate or support action, nationally, or in any part of this nation, by individuals or organizations, to break through the silken curtain of prejudice and discrimination against women in government, industry, the professions, the churches, the political parties, the judiciary, the labor unions, in education, science, medicine, law, religion and every other field of importance in American society.

Enormous changes taking place in our society make it both possible and urgently necessary to advance the unfinished revolution of women toward true equality, now. With a life span lengthened to nearly 75 years it is no longer either necessary or possible for women to devote the greater part of their lives to child-rearing; yet childbearing and rearing which continues to be a most important part of most women's lives—still is used to justify barring women from equal professional and economic participation and advance.

Today's technology has reduced most of the productive chores which women once performed in the home and in mass-production industries based upon routine unskilled labor. This same technology has virtually eliminated the quality of muscular strength as a criterion for filling most jobs, while intensifying American industry's need for creative intelligence. In view of this new industrial revolution created by automation in the mid-twentieth century, women can and must participate in old and new fields of society in full equality—or become permanent outsiders.

Despite all the talk about the status of American women in recent years, the actual position of women in the United States has declined, and is declining, to an alarming degree throughout the 1950's and 60's. Although 46.4% of all American women between the ages of 18 and 65 now work outside the home, the overwhelming majority—75%—are in routine clerical, sales, or factory jobs, or they are household workers, cleaning women, hospital attendants. About two-thirds of Negro women workers are in the lowest paid service occupations. Working women are becoming increasingly—not less—concentrated on the bottom of the job ladder. As a consequence full-time women workers today earn on the average only 60% of what men earn, and that wage gap has been increasing over the past twenty-five years in every major industry group. In 1964, of all women with a yearly income, 89% earned under $5,000 a year; half of all full-time year round women workers earned less than $3,690; only 1.4% of full-time year round women workers had an annual income of $10,000 or more.

Further, with higher education increasingly essential in today's society, too few women are entering and finishing college or going on to graduate or professional school. Today, women earn only one in three of the B.A.'s and M.A.'s granted, and one in ten of the Ph.D.'s.

In all the professions considered of importance to society, and in the executive ranks of industry and government, women are losing ground. Where they are present it is only a token handful. Women comprise less than 1% of federal judges; less than 4% of all lawyers; 7% of doctors. Yet women represent 51% of the U.S. population. And, increasingly, men are replacing women in the top positions in secondary and elementary schools, in social work, and in libraries—once thought to be women's fields.

Official pronouncements of the advance in the status of women hide not only the reality of this dangerous decline, but the fact that nothing is being done to stop it. The excellent reports of the President's Commission on the Status of Women and of the State Commissions have not been fully implemented. Such Commissions have power only to advise. They have no power to enforce their recommendation; nor have they the freedom to organize American women and men to press for action on them. The reports of these commissions have, however, created a basis upon which it is now possible to build. Discrimination in employment on the basis of sex is now prohibited by federal law, in Title VII of the Civil Rights Act of 1964. But although nearly one-third of the cases brought before the Equal Employment Opportunity Commission during the first year dealt with sex discrimination and the proportion is increasing dramatically, the Commission has not made clear its intention to enforce the law with the same seriousness on behalf of women as of other victims of discrimination. Many of these cases were Negro women, who are the victims of double discrimination of race and sex. Until now, too few women's organizations and official spokesmen have been willing to speak out against these dangers facing women. Too many women have been restrained by the fear of being called "feminist." There is no civil rights movement to speak for women, as there has been for Negroes and other victims of discrimination. The National Organization for Women must therefore begin to speak.

WE BELIEVE that the power of American law, and the protection guaranteed by the U.S. Constitution to the civil rights of all individuals, must be effectively applied and enforced to isolate and remove patterns of sex discrimination, to ensure equality of opportunity in employment and education, and equality of civil and political rights and responsibilities on behalf of women, as well as for Negroes and other deprived groups.

We realize that women's problems are linked to many broader questions of social justice; their solution will require concerted action by many groups. Therefore, convinced that human rights for all are indivisible, we expect to give active support to the common cause of equal rights for all those who suffer discrimination and deprivation, and we call upon other organizations committed to such goals to support our efforts toward equality for women.

WE DO NOT ACCEPT the token appointment of a few women to high-level positions in government and industry as a substitute for serious continuing effort to recruit and advance women according to their individual abilities. To this end, we urge American government and industry to mobilize the same resources of ingenuity and command with which they have solved problems of far greater difficulty than those now impeding the progress of women.

WE BELIEVE that this nation has a capacity at least as great as other nations, to innovate new social institutions which will enable women to enjoy the true equality of opportunity and responsibility in society, without conflict with their responsibilities as mothers and homemakers. In such innovations, America does not lead the Western world, but lags by decades behind many European countries. We do not accept the traditional assumption that a woman has to choose between marriage and motherhood, on the one hand, and serious participation in industry or the professions on the other. We question the present expectation that all normal women will retire from job or profession for 10 or 15 years, to devote their full time to raising children, only to reenter the job market at a relatively minor level. This, in itself, is a deterrent to the aspirations of women, to their acceptance into management or professional training courses, and to the very possibility of equality of opportunity or real choice, for all but a few women. Above all, we reject the assumption that these problems are the unique responsibility of each individual woman, rather than a basic social dilemma which society must solve. True equality of opportunity and freedom of choice for women requires such practical, and possible innovations as a nationwide network of child-care centers, which will make it unnecessary for women to retire completely from society until their children are grown, and national programs to provide retraining for women who have chosen to care for their children full-time.

WE BELIEVE that it is as essential for every girl to be educated to her full potential of human ability as it is for every boy—with the knowledge that such education is the key to effective participation in today's economy and that, for a girl as for a boy, education can only be serious where there is expectation that it will be used in society. We believe that American educators are capable of devising means of imparting such expectations to girl students. Moreover, we consider the decline in the proportion of women receiving higher and professional education to be evidence of discrimination. This discrimination may take the form of quotas against the admission of women to colleges, and professional schools; lack of encouragement by parents, counselors and educators; denial of loans or fellowships; or the traditional or arbitrary procedures in graduate and professional training geared in terms of men, which inadvertently discriminate against women. We believe that the same serious attention must be given to high school dropouts who are girls as to boys.

WE REJECT the current assumptions that a man must carry the sole burden of supporting himself, his wife, and family, and that a woman is automatically entitled to lifelong support by a man upon her marriage, or that marriage, home and family are primarily woman's world and responsibility—hers, to dominate—his to support. We believe that a true partnership between the sexes demands a different concept of marriage, an equitable sharing of the responsibilities of home and children and of the economic burdens of their support. We believe that proper recognition should be given to the economic and social value of homemaking and child-care. To these ends, we will seek to open a reexamination of laws and mores governing marriage and divorce, for we believe that the current state of "half-equity" between the sexes discriminates against both men and women, and is the cause of much unnecessary hostility between the sexes.

WE BELIEVE that women must now exercise their political rights and responsibilities as American citizens. They must refuse to be segregated on the basis of sex into separate-and-not-equal ladies' auxiliaries in the political parties, and they must demand representation according to their numbers in the regularly constituted party committees—at local, state, and national levels—and in the informal power structure, participating fully in the selection of candidates and political decision-making, and running for office themselves.

IN THE INTERESTS OF THE HUMAN DIGNITY OF WOMEN, we will protest, and endeavor to change, the false image of women now prevalent in the mass media, and in the texts, ceremonies, laws, and practices of our major social institutions. Such images perpetuate contempt for women by society and by women for themselves. We are similarly opposed to all policies and practices—in church, state, college, factory, or office—which, in the guise of protectiveness, not only deny opportunities but also foster in women self-denigration, dependence, and evasion of responsibility, undermine their confidence in their own abilities and foster contempt for women.

NOW WILL HOLD ITSELF INDEPENDENT OF ANY POLITICAL PARTY in order to mobilize the political power of all women and men intent on our goals. We will strive to ensure that no party, candidate, president, senator, governor, congressman, or any public official who betrays or ignores the principle of full equality between the sexes is elected or appointed to office. If it is necessary to mobilize the votes of men and women who believe in our cause, in order to win for women the final right to be fully free and equal human beings, we so commit ourselves.

WE BELIEVE THAT women will do most to create a new image of women by acting now, and by speaking out in behalf of their own equality, freedom, and human dignity—not in pleas for special privilege, nor in enmity toward men, who are also victims of the current, half-equality between the sexes—but in an active, self-respecting partnership with men. By so doing, women will develop confidence in their own ability to determine actively, in partnership with men, the conditions of their life, their choices, their future and their society.

BIL GILBERT AND NANCY WILLIAMSON

Sport Is Unfair to Women, 1973

Gilbert and Williamson's three-part series on the inequality of women and men's sports was one of the pivotal moments in the emergence of women's sports. Published shortly after the passage of Title IX, this series provided a mountain of statistical evidence to support the notion that educational institutions, the media, and society at large discriminated against women in athletics. The authors offered quote after quote that illustrated men's belief that women should not have an equal seat at the sporting table. By laying bare the assumptions and facts that underlay women's secondary status in athletics, the articles helped both athletes and administrators support their demands for change.

How large was the gap between men and women in the resources and opportunities they enjoyed in athletics? Did women actually want more opportunities? What role do the men quoted in the article reprinted here believe women should play in sports and society? What changes do Gilbert and Williamson seem to support?

This article is critical for all players of the game. By laying out the status of women's athletics before Title IX was implemented, it suggests that legal requirements were necessary to force men to allow women a chance to participate. Supporters of Title IX will want to argue that this demonstrates the need to continue enforcing Title IX. Opponents will suggest that society has moved on and that legal enforcement of women's rights is no longer necessary. In other words, they'll want to argue that the conditions exposed here are not relevant to the current conversation.

SOURCE: *Bil Gilbert and Nancy Williamson,* Sports Illustrated, *May 28, 1973, pp. 88–98.*

*T*here may be worse (more socially serious) forms of prejudice in the United States, but there is no sharper example of discrimination today than that which operates against girls and women who take part in competitive sports, wish to take part, or might wish to if society did not scorn such endeavors. No matter what her age, education, race, talent, residence or riches, the female's right to play is severely restricted. The funds, facilities, coaching, rewards and honors allotted women are grossly inferior to those granted men. In many places absolutely no support is given to women's athletics, and females are barred by law, regulation, tradition or the hostility of males from sharing athletic resources and pleasures. A female who persists in her athletic interests, despite the handicaps and discouragements, is not likely to be congratulated on her sporting desire or grit. She is more apt to be subjected to social and psychological pressures, the effect of which is to cast doubt on her morals, sanity and womanhood.

As things stand, any female—the 11-year-old who is prohibited from being a Little League shortstop by Act of Congress; the coed basketball player who cannot practice in her university's multimillion-dollar gymnasium; the professional sportswoman who can earn only one-quarter what her male counterpart receives for trying to do the same work—has ample reasons for believing that the American system of athletics is sexist and hypocritical. There is a publicly announced, publicly supported notion that sports are good for people, that they develop better citizens, build vigorous minds and bodies and promote a better society. Yet when it comes to the practice of what is preached, females—half this country's population—find that this credo does not apply to them. Sports may be good for people, but they are considered a lot gooder for male people than for female people.

Opportunities for women are so limited that it is a cop-out to designate females as second-class citizens of the American sports world. "Most of us feel that being second-class citizens would be a great advance," says Doris Brown. A faculty member at Seattle Pacific College, Brown has devoted 15 years to becoming the best U.S. female distance runner. She has been on two Olympic teams, won six national and five world cross-country championships and set a variety of national and international records in distances from a mile up. Despite her talent and success she has had to pay for nearly all her training and, until recently, all her travel expenses. She was forced to resign from a job at a junior high school because the principal did not believe in women teachers devoting a lot of time to outside athletic participation. She has received far less recognition than male runners who cannot match her record of accomplishment. "Second-class citizenship sounds good," says Brown, "when you are accustomed to being regarded as fifth-class." This is not the whine of a disgruntled individual but an accurate description of the state of things in sports. To document the situation, consider the following:

MONEY TALKS

- In 1969 a Syracuse, N. Y. school board budgeted $90,000 for extracurricular sports for boys; $200 was set aside for girls. In 1970 the board cut back on the athletic budget, trimming the boy's program to $87,000. Funds for the girls' interscholastic program were simply eliminated.

- New Brunswick (N.J.) Senior High School offered 10 sports for boys and three for girls in 1972, with the split in funds being $25,575 to $2,250 in favor of the boys. The boys' track team was allowed $3,700 last spring, while the girls' squad received $1,000. This might be considered a better-than-average division of money except that 70 New Brunswick students competed on the girls' team and only 20 on the boys'.

- The Fairfield area school district in rural south-central Pennsylvania is small: 800 students are enrolled from kindergarten through 12th grade. Nevertheless, in 1972-73 the school district budgeted $19,880 for interscholastic athletics. Of this $460 was actually spent on girls' sports, $300 of it on a "play day" in the area and $160 on a volleyball team, which had a one-month season. Boys in the school district are introduced to competitive sport as early as the fifth grade with the organization of soccer and basketball teams that are coached by members of the high school athletic staff.

- In New York a woman officiating a girls' high school basketball game is paid $10.50, a man receives $21 for a boys' game. Throughout the country and with few exceptions, women who coach girls' sports in secondary schools receive between one-third and one-half the salary of men who coach comparable sports for boys. The woman coach often is expected to supervise candy sales, cooking contests and raffles to raise money to purchase the girls' uniforms and pay travel expenses.

There are many communities where tax-supported school systems offer absolutely no athletic programs for girls. In fact, until recently no money was spent for girls' interscholastic sports in two entire states—Utah and Nevada.

- In colleges the disparity between men's and women's athletics is even greater than it is in the secondary schools. At the University of Washington, 41.4% of the 26,464 undergraduate students enrolled are women. However, when it comes to athletics women get only nine-tenths of 1% of the $2 million the university spends annually on sports. The women's intercollegiate budget is $18,000 a year. while the men have $1.3 million to spend over and above the income-producing sports of football and basketball. Despite the enormous discrepancy, the situation at Washington has markedly improved. In 1957 there were no women's intercollegiate athletics at the university. Dr. Joseph Kearney, director of sports at Washington, says, "We want to develop the women's programs that are now in an evolutionary stage." Evolutionary is a clinically accurate term. If the *current rate of progress were maintained,* women would reach financial parity with men in the year 2320.

- Things are better at Vassar, but hardly as good as one might expect, considering the college's pioneer role in women's education and rights. In 1968 Vassar admitted male students for the first time. There are now 1,400 girls and 700 boys enrolled. Vassar men compete in five sports and have an annual budget of $4,750. The women have three sports and $2,060 to spend.

- Since its organization in 1910 the National Collegiate Athletic Association has governed men's collegiate athletics. The NCAA now has an annual operating budget of $1.5 million and 42 full-time employees. The female counterpart of the NCAA is the Association for Intercollegiate Athletics for Women. It was established only in 1971. Prior to that, there seemed little need for an organization because there were so few intercollegiate women's programs. The AIAW operates on $24,000 a year and employs one executive (who works part-time) and one assistant.

- In five major collegiate athletic conferences—Southeastern, Big Ten, Big Eight, Southwest and PAC 8—there are 5,000 students on football scholarships alone. These legitimate scholarships (to say nothing of any under-the-table goodies) are worth some $10 million a year to their recipients. Women are almost totally excluded from the scholarship system which, whatever its deficiencies, is the one used to develop most of our first-class athletes. As many as 50,000 men a year earn a college education by playing games. Figures are hard to come by, but it is likely that less than 50 American women hold athletic scholarships and enjoy the benefits—financial, educational, sporting—that these grants provide.

Whatever the small total of women scholarship holders is, it was reduced by one in January 1973 when Cathy Carr, a swimmer who had won two gold medals at the Munich Olympics, had to resign the four-year grant she had been awarded by the University of New Mexico. The reason: she and the astonished university discovered that a woman holding an athletic scholarship was barred from competing in women's intercollegiate events by, of all things, the AIAW.

Recently, Mary Rekstad, the AIAW's lone executive, explained the Alice in Wonderland regulation. "When the AIAW was formed many men told us that scholarships were a bad influence on collegiate sports, that we should avoid making the mistakes they had made and stay out of the mess." On the surface the concern of the admittedly corrupt men for the purity of their female counterparts seems more hilarious than touching—something like a confirmed alcoholic guzzling all the booze at a party to protect the other guests from the evils of drink.

"It might seem that the men were motivated by self-interest," said Rekstad. "But we did not think so. We wanted to protect girls from the excesses of recruiting and exploitation." Last month the AIAW reassessed the situation and decided to drop the regulation. Now women on athletic scholarships can take part in events it sanctions.

- When it comes to pay-for-play situations, unequal scales are established for men and women. As a small but instructive example, one of the leading events of the Northern California tennis circuit is held each May in Mountain View. This tournament is open to men and women and each entrant, regardless of sex, must pay an $8 fee. About an equal number of men and women compete. However, when it comes to prize money, sex raises its miserly head. At Mountain View the men's singles winner receives $1,000, the runner-up $500, the semifinal losers $150 each, quarter-final losers $75 each, and the round of 16 losers $25 each. On the other hand, the women's singles winner receives $150, and the runner-up $50. The women receive no other money prizes. There also is a doubles competition for men, but not for women. In all, though they have put up the same entry fee, $3,000 is paid to men while the women play for $200. In monetary terms, the Mountain View tournament considers women 15th-class citizens.

- In 1971 Billie Jean King became the first woman athlete to win $100,000 in a year. During the same year Rod Laver was the leading winner on the men's tennis circuit, collecting $290,000. To reach her total King won three times as many tournaments as Laver. Last year King captured the U.S. Open at Forest Hills and collected $10,000. Ilie Nastase was the men's winner and earned $25,000. At Wimbledon Stan Smith collected $12,150 for the men's title while King picked up only $4,830 for the women's. At Forest Hills and Wimbledon the women often draw as many spectators, and sometimes more than the men.

- In 1972 on the Ladies Professional Golftour Kathy Whitworth was the leading money-winner, collecting $65,063 in 29 tournaments. In the same year Jack Nicklaus was the biggest moneymaker among the men pros, winning $320,542 in 19 tournaments. The discrepancy between men and women professionals is even more notable among lesser competitors. The 15th leading money-winner on the women's tour in 1972 was JoAnne Carner, who made $18,901. The 15th-place finisher among the men, Jim Jamieson, collected $109,532. Admittedly, the women's tour arouses less interest than the men's, and sponsors feel they receive a better return for their money backing men's events.

- *In the Roller Derby* it is the women, more than the men, who attract fans and generate publicity. The female star of the Derby is Joan Weston, a superior athlete. She makes between $25,000 and $30,000 a year. There are six men on the Derby tour who play the same game in front of the same crowds as Weston, all of whom earn larger salaries. Charlie O'Connell, the leading male performer, is paid twice as much as Weston. When they join the Derby tour, men and women are paid about $85 a week plus travel expenses. But men's salaries increase more rapidly than women's, and once established a man will receive between $200 and $250 a week, while a women of equal talent makes only $150.

BIG BROTHER

- Dr. Katherine Ley, a full professor and chairman of the women's physical education department of the State University College of New York at Cortland, is one of the country's leading physical educators. She long has sought better opportunities for women in sports. At Dr. Ley's university (men's budget $84,000 a year: women's $18,000) the situation could hardly be described as one of sweetness, light and equality. For example, the Cortland women's basketball team cannot practice regularly in the main gymnasium, but it is permitted to play varsity games there. Recently one such game ran overtime whereupon, according to Dr. Ley, the men's basketball coach stormed into the gym and told the girls to get off the court because the boys had to practice. The women's coach asked if he couldn't use the field house, explaining that her team was in the middle of a game and had reserved the space. He said he was in a hurry because he had to leave shortly to scout another team. He told the women it was silly to finish: the score was lopsided and it was not even a game. The women docilely left the game unfinished and withdrew.

- The Mission Conference, an eight-team league of California junior colleges, agreed not long ago that women could compete in varsity sports with and against men. Last February in a game against San Diego City College, Ray Blake, the basketball coach of San Bernardino Valley College, took advantage of the new ruling. Leading 114 to 85 with three minutes and 12 seconds to play, Blake sent in a substitute, Sue Palmer. The San Diego coach, Bill Standly, responded by calling time and asking his men, "Do you want to be humiliated any further by playing against a girl?" The team, to a man, said no, and San Diego walked off the court.

- At a parochial high school in Maryland, a girls' basketball team was playing a varsity rival. The game was officiated by the man who serves as athletic director of the host school. As the contest drew toward a close, the A.D., bored and feeling that he could spend his time better elsewhere, turned to the timekeeper and, in something less than a whisper, suggested that the clock not be stopped for timeouts, that it be kept running until the game ended. One of the players overheard the conversation and said, "That's unfair." "That, young lady, is a technical foul on you," said the athletic director, ending the argument.

THE FEMININE MYSTIQUE

- Ron Wied is the football coach at coed Pius XI in Milwaukee, the largest Catholic high school in the state. Wied says, "There is cause for concern among our male coaching staff over the pressure for girls' sports. Facilities are a problem. We've got a boys' gym and a girls' gym. Before, we could use the girls' gym for wrestling and B team basketball a lot more than we can now. I think girls have a right to participate but to a lesser degree than boys. If they go too far with the competitive stuff they lose their femininity. I guess if I had my choice. I'd like to keep boys' teams going up in importance and let the girls stay about where they are now."

- Jack Short is the director of physical education for the State of Georgia school system. Speaking of the physical education program there, Short commented, "I don't think the idea is to get girls interested in interscholastic competition. I don't think the phys ed program on any level should be directed toward making an athlete of a girl."

- At the Munich Games, Olga Connolly, a female discus thrower, was selected to carry the U.S. flag at the opening ceremonies. Upon learning that Connolly would be the American color-bearer, Russell Knipp, a weight lifter, said, "The flag-bearer ought to be a man, a strong man, a warrior. A woman's place is in the home."

- At Trenton (N.J.) State College the usual man-woman inequality exists, with $70,000 budgeted for men and only $15,687 for women. Joyee Countiss, the women's basketball coach, is paid considerably less than her male counterpart, but as far as she is concerned, the day-to-day discriminations are as humiliating as the monetary inequality. "We aren't supposed to sweat," says Countiss fiercely. "The men's uniforms are laundered by the school, but if we want ours clean we wash them ourselves. We have no athletic trainer: the men have one who even travels with the teams. The school has a training room with whirlpool baths, heat treatments, etc., but women get to use the facilities only in emergencies. The weight room is located in the men's locker room, so naturally we have no access to it. The list goes on and on, but most places are much worse off than we are."

- Susan Hollander is a student at Hamden (Conn.) High School. She had sufficient talent to be a member of her school's varsity cross-country and indoor track teams. There was no girls' team, and she was prohibited by a state regulation from participating on the boys' team. Backed by her parents, she brought suit against the Connecticut Interscholastic Athletic Conference. The case was heard on March 29, 1971 in the Superior Court of New Haven and Judge John Clark FitzGerald ruled against Hollander. In giving his decision Judge FitzGerald stated, "The present generation of our younger male population has not become so decadent that boys will experience a thrill in defeating girls in running contests, whether the girls be members of their own team or of an adversary team. It could well be that many boys would feel compelled to forgo entering track events if they were required to compete with girls on their own teams or on adversary teams. With boys vying with girls . . . the challenge to win, and the glory of achievement, at least for many boys, would lose incentive and become nullified. Athletic competition builds character in our boys. We do not need that kind of character in our girls."

- John Roberts, the executive secretary of the Wisconsin Interscholastic Athletic Association, says many coaches of boys' teams in his state are worried about the increased interest in girls' sports. "The facilities thing will get worse," says one of Roberts' colleagues. "Girls haven't figured out yet how to use the urinals."

THE DOUBLE STANDARD

- Last summer a steward at Ellis Park in Kentucky sought to suspend Jockey Mary Bacon for cursing in the paddock after a losing ride. Said Bacon, "They expect a girl to get off a horse and say. 'Nice horsey, nice horsey,' like in *National Velvet*. Well, I get mad like everyone else. If I lost a race and didn't cuss, then the stewards might have something to worry about."

- When asked why only women were permitted to coach girls' teams, Ada Mae Warrington, director of physical education for women in the Prince George's County (Md.) school system, said, "We have had several instances of a girl assaulting a man. We are trying to protect our coaches."

- In 1971, after a lengthy argument with the New York State Education Department, Katy Schilly was permitted to run on the Paul V. Moore High School cross-country team. After the decision was made, an elaborate security system was set up to protect her. Among other things, a woman had to be present whenever the runner was in her locker room. "Maybe they're afraid I'll slip on a bar of soap in the shower," said Schilly.

Prudery is a major factor contributing to the present low estate of women's sports. This hangup cannot be blamed on our Victorian or Puritan ancestors. Early in this century there was widespread participation by girls in competitive athletics. Baseball, bike racing and track and field were popular pastimes for girls. Basketball was played extensively, and often girls' games were scheduled as doubleheaders with boys' contests. Then in 1923, a national committee of women headed by Mrs. Herbert Hoover was formed to investigate the practice of holding such doubleheaders. The committee was shocked to find girls wearing athletic costumes performing before crowds that included men. Mrs. Hoover and her friends believed the girls were being used as a come-on and that the practice was disgraceful and should be stopped. State after state followed the advice and either abolished all girls' sports or made them so genteel as to be almost unrecognizable as athletic contests.

"When I went to college in the '30s, we were taught that competition was dirty," recalls Betty Desch, head of the women's physical education department of the State University of New York at Stony Brook. Those states that had retained any girls' athletic programs declared that teams should be coached only by women, or else who knows what might transpire. The requirement, still in effect in many states, has stifled the development of competent female athletic programs. While there is no evidence that women cannot be as good coaches as men, it is a fact that there are very few good women coaches. There are obvious reasons for this. Few girls in high school or college have had the same competitive opportunities as men, so they are seldom inspired to take up coaching as a career. Also, few colleges allow girls to take courses in coaching techniques and theory. Where they can attend such classes, there has been little point in doing so, since once a girl graduates she finds few coaching jobs available, and those that are available pay poorly or not at all. When a school needs a coach for a girls' team, the usual practice is to draft a woman from the physical education department for the job. Through no fault of her own, she rarely has much expertise or enthusiasm for coaching competitive athletics. In consequence, girls in her charge do not learn fundamental techniques, skills and seldom become excited about athletics. Thus the vicious circle is continued.

THE SAME OLD STORY

The following letter appeared not long ago in *The Washington Post*:

"Your editorial, 'Growing Up by the Book' (Dec. 1), revealed the harmful effects of stereotyped sex roles in children's books and toys. But it seems that *The Washington Post* is extending this same discrimination to its sports pages.

"Our specific complaint is that girls' high school basketball scores are completely ignored in your paper while boys' high school basketball is given 500-word articles. There are numerous active, aggressive teams from all-girls' schools as well as public schools. Girls' basketball is not a farce: it is an exciting spectator sport with a four-month season that is of interest to thousands of Washington-area students, including boys.

"We suggest that you 'practice what you preach' and print reports on a sport where girls are anything but passive."

- The amount of coverage given to women's athletics is meager and the quality is atrocious. Most of the stories that do appear are generally in the man-bites-dog journalistic tradition, the gist of them being that here is an unusual and mildly humorous happening—a girl playing games. Rather than describing how well or badly the athlete performed or even how the contest turned out, writers tend to concentrate on the color of the hair and eyes, and the shape of the legs or the busts of the women. The best-looking girls (by male standards) are singled out for attention, no matter how little their sporting talent may be. Women athletes are bothered by this, since the insinuation is "at least some of them look normal." It is comparable to a third-string defensive back being featured on a college football program cover because of the length of his eyelashes or the symmetry of his profile.

- A fine (in the sense of being typical) example of women's sports journalism appeared in the Aug. 23, 1971 issue of SPORTS ILLUSTRATED: "A cool, braided California blonde named Laura Baugh made quite a splash . . . her perfectly tanned, well-formed legs swinging jauntily. The hair on her tapered arms was bleached absolutely white against a milk-chocolate tan. Her platinum hair was pulled smartly back in a

Viking-maiden braid. . . ." The account had to do with a women's golf tournament. The difference in reporting men's and women's sporting events is obvious.

• Between August 1972 and September 1973 NBC will televise 366 hours of "live" sport. Only one hour of this (the finals at Wimbledon) will be devoted to women. Til Ferdenzi, manager of sports publicity for NBC says, "Egad. I never thought about it before. I guess it's not fair." Bill Brendle, his counterpart at CBS, says, "We don't know if women draw an audience they might not be saleable." During the coming year CBS will televise some 260 hours of men's sports and 10 hours of women's sports. ABC does not know how its time is divided between men and women athletes, but ABC's Irv Brodsky says defensively, "Women don't play sports."

The paucity and peculiarity of sporting news about females have two effects, both discriminatory. First, girls at all levels of play are deprived of the genuine and harmless satisfaction of seeing their athletic accomplishments publicized. Because the feats of outstanding women athletes are briefly and bizarrely reported, there are few sporting heroines. Boys are bombarded with daily stories about how much fun male athletes are having, how important, dashing and rich they are. The suggestion is made that getting out and playing games—and playing them well—is an exciting and constructive thing to do. Girls have few such models and seldom receive such subliminal messages advertising athletics.

In an informal survey taken for the purposes of this report, nearly all of some 100 high school girls scattered across the country could name 10 male athletes in college or professional sports whom they admired or at least whose names they knew. But not a single girl to whom the question was put could name 10 prominent women athletes. The sportswoman most often identified by the high school girls was not an American but Olga Korbut, the 17-year-old Russian gymnast (SI cover, Mar. 19) who appeared prominently on television during the 1972 Olympics.

As bad as it is, conventional discrimination has perhaps had less influence on women's position in the sporting world than has another phenomenon that ranges even further. It might be called psychological warfare: its purpose is to convince girls who show an inclination for athletics that their interest is impractical and unnatural. The campaign to frighten girls into accepting notions about their athletic role begins early

Carol is 12, an eighth-grade student at a parochial grammar school in Maryland. She is one of the best athletes, regardless of sex, in the school. Last year she was ranked by the AAU among the 15 best high jumpers of her age in the country. She comes by her athletic interests and talents naturally. Her father was a professional basketball player and now is a college coach. In her family, playing games is a way of life. But Carol is discovering that elsewhere sports are not regarded as suitable for girls. And it makes her angry. "At recess," Carol says, "the boys get the softball and kickball fields. The girls have a parking lot and part of a field with holes in it. Sometimes we don't even get that field because Sister keeps us in to wash off tables. She says that is girls' work."

C.M. Russell High School in Great Falls, Mont. has 2,040 students and an excellent girls' athletic program ($15,000 a year for girls; $35,000 for boys). Yet even there, the members of a six-girl panel discussing sports were aware of forces putting them in their athletic place.

"There's one thing that really doesn't have anything to do with school," said one girl. "If you've got a brother and he's playing football or basketball your folks are going to drive him back and forth to practice and change dinner hours for him. But if you're a girl, your mother says, 'Be home at 5 to set the table.'"

Early on, girls learn to expect and put up with parental edicts and insinuations that the games they play are unimportant. When she is 15 or 16 the campaign against a girl's athletic interest takes an uglier turn, being directed against her appearance and sexuality. The six C.M. Russell girls were attractive teen-agers. Most of them dated boys who were athletes. "The guys on the teams tease us about being jocks," said a tiny lithe gymnast, "but they are just having fun. They know we work hard and I think they are proud of what we do."

"The mean ones," said a basketball player, "are those who aren't in sports themselves. They don't want to see a girl play because it makes them look bad. They want her to sit in the stands with them. So they try to put us down. They'll come up in the hall and give you an elbow and say, 'Hey, stud.'"

"Some girls are bad, too," a hurdler noted. "They'll say, 'Aren't you afraid you'll get ugly muscles in your legs?'"

"Girls in sports are more careful about how they look," said the gymnast. "We wear skirts more than other girls because we are worried about being feminine."

Some authorities consider the word "feminine" a derogatory term. "When we say 'feminine,'" says Dr. David Auster of Slippery Rock State College, "we mean submissive, a nonparticipant, an underachiever, a person who lacks a strong sense of self-identity, who has weak life goals and ambitions."

Grosse Pointe (Mich.) North High School has a far different and lesser girls' sports program than that of C.M. Russell in Montana. There are two official girls' interscholastic sports, gymnastics and track. There are financed by a $2,200, hopefully annual, grant from a local boosters club. In contrast, boys receive about $20,000 in school funds. But in at least one respect girl athletes are treated better at Grosse Pointe than in many other places. Girls are awarded school letters that they may wear on a sweater. In many other localities, players are rewarded with inconspicuous pins, printed certificates, or nothing. In practice, winning and being able to wear a letter sweater is an empty honor for Grosse Pointe girls. "Not very many girls wear their letter," says Pam Candler, a senior who is the Michigan girls' trampoline champion and was runner-up last spring in the state tennis championships. "Mostly only freshmen or sophomores—because they don't know what the score is."

What is the score?

"Well, a lot of people think it is freakish for a girl to wear a letter sweater. Like she's a jock. I'm kind of proud of the girls who have enough courage to wear them, but I don't. It would make me feel funny. I guess I've been brainwashed."

"I don't like to think that there are male chauvinists, but I guess there are," says Jan Charvat, another gymnast. "It is degrading that we have to act in a certain way just because we're in sports. A girl ought to be free to be what she is, without people cutting her up."

So far as the "social" acceptability of girls' sports at Grosse Pointe, Candler says, "If a girl is great looking, then maybe the guy she is going with likes to see her in sports. If she isn't good looking and popular, sports are not going to help her. In fact they will do the opposite."

Bruce Feighner, the principal of Grosse Pointe North, is not proud of the weakness of his girls' athletic program. However, like so many of his colleagues, he cites the lack of funds as a major reason for the inequality: "Here and in many other communities in Michigan, taxpayer revolts are brewing. It is hard to establish new programs. This admittedly is unjust, but the fault is not entirely or perhaps even principally with the school. The role of girls in sport is determined by society, and until now that role has been an inferior one. There's another practical side to the matter. Grosse Pointe is a very affluent community. If a girl is interested in athletics, the conventional way of developing her skill is to marry a man who has enough money to belong to a country club, a tennis or yacht club."

Feighner's comment may seem cynical but it is perceptive. Except occasionally in track (where the leading female performers are developed in private AAU clubs) the only women's sports in which the U.S. record is respectable, occasionally outstanding, are tennis, golf, skating, skiing and swimming, essentially country-club sports and ones that are considered "ladylike." For the girl who lacks country-club opportunities and inclinations, yet somehow has kept her interest in athletics through high school, the question of what to do next is perplexing. For men, the next stage in the American athletic progression is college, where sporting skills are polished and reputations made. However, college sports presently have little attraction or value for good female athletes.

The woman athlete at the university is made to feel unwelcome and an oddity. Beth Miller is a tall, graceful 21-year-old, by any standards a figure pleasing to the eye. She is also one of the best female athletes in the country, having been the National Junior Women's pentathlon and shotput champion, a standout performer on her Lock Haven (Pa.) State College basketball team, a swimmer, softball player and spelunker. On one weekend last winter, Miller led her basketball team to victory and then hurried to Baltimore where she won the shotput and placed third in the high jump at an AAU indoor meet. Word of her accomplishments was received by a Lock Haven radio sportscaster. The commentator spent maybe 20 seconds describing what Miller had done and ended with the comment, "What an animal she must be."

If a talented woman withstands these pressures and decides to become a serious athlete, she often has to cope not just with insinuations but with slanderous gossip. Jo Ann Prentice is a sharp-tongued, sharp-minded woman who has earned her living for 17 years on the LPGA tour. Asked about the "social" life on the tour, Prentice replied to the euphemistic question in her soft Alabama drawl. "This is kind of how it is. If you get into town at the beginning of the week and you meet some guy whose company you enjoy and have dinner with him once or twice, the gossips start asking what kind of tramps are these babes on the tour. If you stay at the motel where everybody else on the tour has checked in, then the question is what are those girls doing back in those rooms alone."

The vicious paradox that Prentice outlines—women athletes are either heterosexual wantons or homosexual perverts or, simultaneously, both—is the culmination of all the jokes and warnings that began when an 11-year-old wanted to play sandlot football with her brothers and was teased, in good fun, about being a tomboy.

As a result, a great many girls simply avoid sports completely. Others try to compromise, accommodating their athletic desires to the attitudes of society. They continue to play games, but play them nervously and timidly, attempting to avoid appearances and enthusiasms that might be construed as unladylike.

The few women who survive the pressure may be scarred in various ways, but there are compensations. Jack Griffin, though he has worked for 25 years in relative obscurity, is regarded by many who know of him as one of the most distinguished athletic coaches in the nation. He has coached boys and girls, from grade-schoolers to post-collegians, in swimming, track, basketball and football. Working only with the youth of the small Maryland city, Frederick, he has helped to develop an inordinate number of national and international class athletes. He has been an Olympic coach and is currently a member of the Olympic Women's Track and Field Committee. "I enjoy coaching both sexes," says Griffin, "but strictly from a coaching standpoint, I have noted one important difference between them. Desire is an intangible quality which you like to see in any athlete. Coaches of men's teams often single out an individual athlete and say his most valuable characteristic is his desire. You seldom hear girls' coaches make this sort of comment. The reason, I think, is that *any* girl or woman who is very much involved in athletics tends to have an extraordinary amount of desire, not only to excel in her sport but to excel as a person. It is so common with the girls that we tend to overlook it, accepting it as normal. I suppose in a sense it is normal for them. The way things are in this country, any girl who perseveres in sport has to be not only an exceptional athlete but an exceptional human being."

BRENDA FEIGEN

Give Women a Sporting Chance, 1973

Women (and many men) justly celebrated the passage of Title IX in 1972. However, the law itself only laid out the principle of equal rights. It didn't define what equality meant, or how to achieve this equality, or whether certain kinds of equality of opportunity might actually further limit opportunities for women.

Throughout the succeeding decade, women (and many men) explored these questions. Should men and women be allowed to try out for the same team? Were there sports that were simply too dangerous (too rough, too physical) for women to play? Should women and men play on the same team?

Over time, a consensus (but never unanimity) emerged. Separate but equal, now considered illegal and unethical in regard to race, was the only way to allow women equal opportunity. Writers disagreed about whether women should be allowed to try out for football (since there was no female equivalent). But they agreed that allowing women and men to try out on the basis of talent for the same team would dramatically diminish opportunities for women.

The article reprinted here is an example of this literature. It's short and meant for a popular audience. If you have a role that addresses these questions (as many do), you'll need to look further (see your role sheet for guidance). But this is a good place to start.

What is the basic question Feigen is asking? Does she believe women and men are biologically equal? The same? What does she believe is the best way to ensure women a fair chance to participate in sports? Why is this important?

SOURCE: Ms. Magazine, *July 1973, pp. 56–58, 103.*

*F*or the first few weeks of the season, two eight-year-old girls longingly watched the practice sessions of a Montgomery, Alabama, boys' football team. Finally, the coach broke down and let them play—but just for one season. I admire the stubbornness and audacity of these two little girls. I am also angry and sad that the same obstacles face them that faced me 20 years ago—when I was their age.

I wonder if they wish, as I once did, that they were boys. When you're that young, it's hard to see the value of being female because boys are permitted to do almost everything girls do, but not vice versa. It is especially hard when you love climbing trees and playing games, but are expected to play with dolls instead.

At about 13 years of age, it becomes even more painful, as boys, almost overnight, seem to grow stronger and bigger than girls. Although I was fairly good at sports and was on the girls' varsity field hockey, basketball, softball, and tennis teams, I was never as good as the best boys. It was small consolation that I was better at some sports—horseback riding and water-skiing. (Perhaps because these sports weren't as popular with boys.)

In athletics as we know them, the average man will probably beat the better-than-average woman. Scientists chalk it up to testosterone and the retention of nitrogen in men's muscles, which make them bigger and bulgier than women's. Even if this is true, the unhappy fact is that sports have been designed for men's rather than women's bodies—which means the emphasis is on strength. We have yet to see major promotion of sports utilizing women's unique flexibility (because of our less bulgy muscles) and better balance (as a result of our lower center of gravity). Gymnastics is the only widely practiced sport where women can outperform their male counterparts—especially on the balance team.

I still haven't fully accepted what it means to be smaller and weaker than most men. From a practical point of view, it shouldn't matter; but it always has inhibited my activities in ways that make strength and sex matter a great deal. For example, in college I learned to play squash. When I got to law school, I discovered that women were banned from the university's squash courts. By disguising myself as a man, I managed to invade the courts with a classmate who is now my husband. We had fun, but I never beat him.

Still, as I remind myself, that may have been as much a matter of opportunity as biology: he's been able to play squash whenever he's wanted to and on courts where I wasn't allowed because of my sex.

Exclusion of women in sports is a concrete and difficult problem. But most young women never even reach the point of challenging their exclusion from their college's athletic facilities or varsity teams. By that time, they have been well conditioned to think of gym as a drag—often doing dancing and exercises, instead of playing football, soccer, basketball, and baseball. From early childhood on, girls are discouraged from taking pride in active and strenuous use of their bodies; boys, meanwhile, are encouraged to get "into condition," to enjoy their athletic ability.

Then there are the subtle discouragements: the unenlightened suspicion that a woman's interest in athletics violates the docile female stereotype and indicates lesbianism (remember the rumors about gym teachers?); the insinuation that if she shows too much interest in sports she may not be able to catch a man; and the general scoffing at women's athletic achievements. One Chicago high school teacher points to clearcut evidence of sex discrimination in sports. "In the latest edition of the school paper, there were five articles on football and no mention at all of the girls' tennis team which had won its last three matches."

I don't mean to suggest that sports should become for women what they have been for many men: a display of aggression, a proof of toughness, and a kind of primitive communication that replaces emotional intimacy. Sweating, swearing, and grunting together as they play, men manage to create a fellowship which they find hard to sustain elsewhere. And sports provide men with yet another vehicle to test domination and preeminence. ("Let the best man win.")

Women, however, often do communicate with each other in noncompetitive, nonathletic situations; they are generally better able to express emotion, and seem to care less about beating each other into submission. Our self-images (unless we are professional athletes) aren't much affected by winning a tennis match. While this may reveal something positive, it also unfortunately indicates that women are conditioned not to take themselves seriously in sports.

Of course, the majority of men do not take the sportswoman seriously, either. I notice that whenever I'm interested in playing tennis with a male partner, no matter how well matched we might be, he invariably prefers to play against another man no better than I. Partly, this reflects his fear of losing to a mere woman. But, in a deeper sense, playing with another man seems to reinforce his own competitive sense of masculinity. If he beats another man, he's somehow more of a man himself. If he beats me, it's irrelevant, predictable. Losing is a blow to his ego whether it's to me or a man, but it's a diversion to play with me; the real contest is man-to-man combat.

However, there are encouraging signs that participation in sports is becoming important to women of all ages. Women are beginning to demand their rights as athletes. In New Jersey, for instance, the State Division on Civil Rights found probable cause in a case brought by a local National Organization for Women chapter because girls were barred from the all-boy Little League team. Most often, sex discrimination charges are filed when girls want to engage in a particular sport which a school offers only to boys. Lawsuits or the threat of legal action have led many schools to accept girls on boys' teams, especially in noncontact sports.

One of the highest courts to rule on the issue of integrating high school teams on the basis of sex is the U.S. Court of Appeals for the Sixth Circuit. In the case of *Morris v. Michigan High School Athletic Association* last January, that court affirmed a lower court order that girls may not be prevented from participating fully in interscholastic noncontact athletics. As a result of the desire of Cynthia Morris and Emily Barrett to participate in interscholastic tennis matches, many high school girls have benefited. In addition, after this complaint was filed, the Michigan Legislature enacted a law guaranteeing that all female pupils be permitted to participate in noncontact interscholastic athletic activities and to compete for a position on the boys' team even if a girls' team exists.

New York and New Mexico now also have new regulations which call for the integration of the sexes in all noncontact sports wherever there is a high school team for boys but not for girls. And lawyers of the American Civil Liberties Union have caused at least five other states—Connecticut, New Jersey, Indiana, Minnesota, and Nebraska—to integrate noncontact sports in their high schools. As a result of litigation, female track stars in Connecticut and Minnesota have made their way onto the men's teams. A young Minnesota woman is now on the boys' skiing team of her high school; another has joined the boys' tennis team of hers.

The Indiana Supreme Court, responding favorably to a class action by a female high school student wishing to play on the boys' golf team, held that the Indiana High School Athletic Association rule against "mixed" participation in noncontact sports was a denial of equal protection under the 14th Amendment to the United States Constitution. (Any institution receiving federal or state money may be in violation of the equal protection clause of the 14th Amendment if it discriminates against women students and coaches in athletic programs; sex discrimination in schools which receive federal funds also violates the Education Amendments of 1972 which recently became federal law.)

In New Jersey a high school sophomore successfully challenged a rule of the state Interscholastic Athletic Association that prohibited high school women from competing on varsity tennis teams. A pilot program has begun in New Jersey to allow girls to compete with boys for positions on varsity teams and to encourage schools to upgrade physical education programs for girls. Specifically, the ruling makes clear that outstanding female athletes receive opportunities for training and competition at their ability levels. Lawsuits have also been won in Louisiana and Oklahoma.

In many of these cases there are no girls' teams, so it's easy to decide that interested girls must be allowed to play with the boys. It is more difficult to resolve the question where a girls' team and a boys' team exist for the same sport. If the highly talented girl athlete is encouraged to join the boys' team at the high school level, why not at the college level? Or in the Olympics and other amateur athletic competition? And if at the Olympics, why not in professional sports?

Unfortunately, no American woman would have made the Olympics if the team had been integrated and if the same criteria for selection were applied to both sexes. The very best men—the ones who enter the Olympic tryouts—are still better than the very best women. And certainly at the professional level, women in direct competition with top men would be in trouble in almost every sport. It is debatable whether Billie Jean King, the Number One woman tennis player in the world, would even make the top 10 if male and female professional tennis players competed against each other.

At the professional level, the point is occasionally made that because women aren't as good as men, the purse in women's tournaments is legitimately smaller. This argument overlooks the fact that women pros, such as Ms. King in tennis, draw crowds just as large if not larger than the men they can't beat and that such women regularly capture the headlines in sports columns.

In any high school or college, integrating teams on an "ability only" basis could result in a new form of exclusion for women players. It would effectively eliminate all opportunities for them to play in organized coached competition.

Obviously, therefore, school athletic training programs have to be developed to balance the scales, and equal financial attention must be paid to both sexes. To begin with the human resource, coaches of women's teams must be paid as much as coaches of men's teams. A woman high school basketball coach recently produced figures showing an allocation by the Syracuse Board of Education of $98,000 for male coaches and $200 for female coaches. Discrepancies between women's and men's salaries may violate not only the 14th Amendment to the Constitution but virtually every piece of legislation in the area of sex discrimination in employment and education. Scholarships, too, must be equalized. The first and, it seems, the only university to establish an athletic scholarship for women is the University of Chicago.

As for the students themselves, Minnesota and Utah lawsuits are asking that equal resources—money and personnel—be devoted to physical education for girls and boys. From the first grade through college, girls and boys should have gym classes together with equal access to athletic facilities and instruction. Students, regardless of sex, should be encouraged to perform to the best of their individual ability.

Until puberty, there are insufficient height or strength differences between girls and boys to justify predominately female or male sports below the junior high school level. Girls and boys from an early age should be taught judo or other skills which convey a sense of their own individual strength and agility. If at some point girls and boys prefer different sports, they can individually separate themselves according to these preferences.

Until there is a relaxation of the external cultural pressure for males to prove their masculinity, boys may well choose sports like football, wrestling, and boxing. In any case, a girl wanting to play football should be permitted to try out for the boys' team if an entire girls' team cannot be formed. Girls with the skills to make the boys' team should have the opportunity to play. I am now arguing in court for the right of a woman student at City College in New York to participate in a men's basketball course because there is none offered for women.

That only noncontact sports are considered suitable for sex-integration is nonsensical. As one proponent for the integration of contact sports puts it: "If we are worried about girls' breasts and internal organs, then give them chest and belly protectors. We haven't spared our male football players any expense in that department. We can't declare that because we think many or even most girls cannot or will not play in certain sports that *none* may therefore be allowed to." To match this myth about women's participation in contact sports, there is also a long-standing controversy over the definition of "contact sports." (Baseball and basketball are considered contact sports.)

Because girls have not enjoyed the same physical and psychological opportunities as boys to develop athletically, I believe that resources must be made available for at least two interscholastic teams per sport: one for girls and one for boys. While sex-segregated teams may sound like the long-discredited separate-but-equal doctrine, it is through a process of careful elimination that this policy emerges as the most viable. The four other alternatives listed below are simply *not* equitable:

1. A system involving ability-determined first-and second-string teams will undoubtedly result in two mostly male teams and no greatly increased participation for females.

2. A first-string team that is sex-integrated to absorb top talent of both sexes plus a second-string all-girl team would increase girls' participation but it runs afoul of boys' rights by excluding them from the second team.

3. If the first-string team is based solely on ability and the second-string team members are evenly divided, boys and girls, the system ends up favoring boys again by assuring them representation on what amounts to one and one-half out of two teams.

4. The quota solution requiring half boys and half girls presents both practical and psychological problems: intrateam ostracizing of the girls who dilute the overall performance, and interteam exploitation of the "weaker" sex members of the opposing team.

So we're left with the separate-but-equal solution. While it may penalize the outstanding female athlete who must play on girls' teams regardless of whether she qualifies for the boys' team, it has the singular advantage of giving boys and girls an equal opportunity to compete interscholastically. This is, in my view, an adequate response to the argument that in sports, as in other areas, women should be compensated for past discriminations. The contention that women should be allowed to try out for men's teams, even if there are comparable women's teams, is potentially unfair to the men who can't make the men's teams but might make the women's teams. Even more importantly, it cheats the women's team which would lose its best athletes to the male squads, thus setting women's sports back even farther.

Where girls' sports are taken seriously at the high school and college level, the results are striking. Throughout Iowa, for instance, girls' basketball draws the bigger crowds. The coaching is excellent, and the facilities and equipment are first-rate. Because women's basketball is a matter of state pride, high school and college women in Iowa eagerly try out without feeling the traditional stigma and scorn so frequently associated with women's sports.

Marcia Federbush of Michigan suggests an Olympic-style system to solve the inevitable imbalance of participation, resource allocation and spectator interest: the girls' varsity and the boys' varsity would *together* constitute the school's varsity team. On the same day or evening both teams would play their counterparts from another school (alternating the game order since the second game is inevitably the star attraction). At the end of the two games the point scores would be totaled. If the boys' basketball squad won 75-70 and the girls' basketball team lost with a score of 60-80, the final school score would amount to a 15-point loss.

The girls' and boys' teams would travel together and use the same facilities. They would enjoy equally skilled (and equally paid) coaching staffs, equal budgets, game schedules, uniforms, equipment, combined publicity attention, and a shared spotlight.

Clearly, when interdependence leads to team success, the primary advantage would be the shared commitment in *two* strong separate-but-equal teams.

DEPARTMENT OF HEALTH, EDUCATION, AND WELFARE

Policy Interpretation: Title IX and Intercollegiate Athletics, 1979

The 1979 Title IX policy interpretation offered a definitive set of standards the government and educational institutions could use to determine whether schools were meeting the requirements of the law. Issued seven years after Title IX was passed, these standards were the result of extensive negotiations (and arguments) among various players in the politics of sports and gender.

How can a university prove that it is meeting Title IX requirements? Does Title IX require equality of spending? An equal number of teams for men and women?

Even after the three-year transition, questions still remained about what constituted compliance. HEW therefore issued this policy interpretation on December 11, 1979, to provide additional guidance. (It was designed for intercollegiate athletics, but HEW noted that the principles also applied to club, intramural, and interscholastic programs.) The major significance of this policy interpretation was the articulation of what came to be known as the "three-prong test." Under this test, an institution could be deemed in compliance with Title IX if it met any one of these three prongs. Not surprisingly, institutions, government investigators, and individual athletes often had different interpretations of how well a specific school was meeting the needs of women athletes, leading to further delays and more recrimination over the implementation of the law.

SOURCE: *U.S. Department of Education, Federal Register, Vol. 44, No. 239, December 11, 1979.*

* * *

5. APPLICATION OF THE POLICY—LEVELS OF COMPETITION

*I*n effectively accommodating the interests and abilities of male and female athletes, institutions must provide both the opportunity for individuals of each sex to participate in intercollegiate competition, and for athletes of each sex to have competitive team schedules which equally reflect their abilities.

a. Compliance will be assessed in any one of the following ways:

(1) Whether intercollegiate level participation opportunities for male and female students are provided in numbers substantially proportionate to their respective enrollment; or

(2) Where the members of one sex have been and are underrepresented among intercollegiate athletes, whether the institution can show a history and continuing practice of program expansion which is demonstrably responsive to the developing interest and abilities of the members of that sex; or

(3) Where the members of one sex are underrepresented among intercollegiate athletes, and the institution cannot show a continuing practice of program expansion such as that cited above, whether it can be demonstrated that the interests and abilities of the members of that sex have been fully and effectively accommodated by the present program.

b. Compliance with this provision of the regulation will also be assessed by examining the following:

(1) Whether the competitive schedules for men's and women's teams, on a program-wide basis, afford proportionally similar numbers of male and female athletes equivalently advanced competitive opportunities; or

(2) Whether the institution can demonstrate a history and continuing practice of upgrading the competitive opportunities available to the historically disadvantaged sex as warranted by developing abilities among the athletes of that sex.

c. Institutions are not required to upgrade teams to intercollegiate status or otherwise develop intercollegiate sports absent a reasonable expectation that intercollegiate competition in that sport will be available within the institution's normal competitive regions. Institutions may be required by the Title IX regulation to actively encourage the development of such competition, however, when overall athletic opportunities within that region have been historically limited for the members of one sex.

6. OVERALL DETERMINATION OF COMPLIANCE

The Department will base its compliance determination under § 88.41 (c) of the regulation upon a determination of the following:

a. Whether the policies of an institution are discriminatory in language or effect; or

b. Whether disparities of a substantial and unjustified nature in the benefits, treatment, services, or opportunities afforded male and female athletes exist in the institution's program as a whole; or

c. Whether disparities in individual segments of the program with respect to benefits, treatment, services, or opportunities are substantial enough in and of themselves to deny equality of athletic opportunity.

* * *

R. VIVIAN ACOSTA AND LINDA CARPENTER

Women in Intercollegiate Sport: A Longitudinal, National Study: Thirty-Seven Year Update, 2014

Acosta and Carpenter yearly compile a statistical report about the status of women in high school, college and university athletics. The data here are compiled from their reports to make it easier for you to use. If you want to go further, feel free to look at the individual reports.

To what degree have women received increased opportunities for athletic participation since the passage of Title IX? Was that increase gradual? Or was there a period where participation opportunities spiked? If so, when? How did the passage of Title IX (or, perhaps, the way it was implemented) shape opportunities for female coaches and administrators?

SOURCE: *Data courtesy of Dr. Vivian Acosta and Dr. Linda Jean Carpenter, Professors Emerita, Brooklyn College, http://acostacarpenter.org*

AVERAGE NUMBER OF WOMEN'S VARSITY TEAMS PER SCHOOL

1970	2.50
1978*	5.61
1979	6.25
1980	6.48
1981	6.46
1982	6.59
1983	6.25
1984	6.90
1985	6.99
1986	7.15
1987	7.24
1988	7.31
1989	7.19
1990	7.25
1991	7.00
1992	7.09
1993	7.02
1994	7.22

*Year of mandatory Title IX compliance.

AVERAGE NUMBER OF WOMEN'S VARSITY TEAMS PER SCHOOL, BY DIVISION

YEAR	DIVISION 1	DIVISION 2	DIVISION 3
1991	7.56	5.76	7.30
1992	7.68	5.74	7.42
1993	7.66	5.68	7.43
1994	7.89	5.81	7.65

PARTICIPATION OPPORTUNITIES FOR FEMALE ATHLETES BY SPORT, 1978 – 1990, ALL DIVISIONS

Percentage of Schools That Offer Each Sport

	1990	1989	1988	1987	1986	1985	1984	1983	1982	1981	1980	1979	1978
Archery	0.8	0.8	1.1	1.2	0.8	0.8	1.2	1.6	1.8	2.2	2.8	3.3	3.0
Badminton	1.0	1.5	1.1	1.2	2.0	2.0	1.9	2.0	3.6	4.4	5.4	6.1	5.9
Basketball	96.2	96.2	97.0	97.2	97.1	96.8	95.5	93.8	97.3	95.9	97.5	96.4	90.4
Bowling	0.8	0.8	1.6	1.9	2.0	2.0	1.9	1.9	2.9	3.3	3.6	3.6	3.4
Crew/rowing	10.5	10.4	11.1	10.9	8.4	8.1	6.9	7.0	7.4	7.7	7.2	6.9	6.9
Cross country	82.1	82.2	82.4	80.1	78.5	75.2	64.0	59.9	59.5	54.0	46.6	39.6	29.4
Fencing	7.4	7.4	9.2	9.5	8.8	9.1	8.0	8.0	10.4	9.8	9.6	9.5	9.8
Field hockey	29.4	29.9	32.6	33.5	34.8	35.5	30.2	30.3	34.6	36.1	37.1	38.2	36.3
Golf	25.8	25.0	24.3	22.5	24.5	23.0	20.5	19.8	19.7	18.5	24.1	20.8	19.9
Gymnastics	15.5	16.0	16.8	17.5	20.6	20.4	18.6	20.0	22.1	23.0	25.6	28.2	25.9
Ice hockey	2.6	2.6	3.0	3.2	2.5	2.7	2.8	2.4	2.9	2.9	1.8	1.5	1.3
Lacrosse	16.9	16.9	18.3	18.2	16.9	17.1	13.5	13.3	13.5	13.7	13.9	13.8	13.0
Riding/equestrian	3.5	3.5	2.6	2.6	2.7	2.4	2.6	2.4	2.4	2.2	3.1	2.5	2.0
Riflery	2.6	3.2	2.6	3.2	4.2	4.2	2.8	2.7	1.8	1.9	3.4	3.3	3.8
Sailing	4.0	3.8	3.4	3.2	2.9	2.7	2.7	2.8	2.7	2.4	1.9	2.5	2.3
Skiing	5.3	5.3	5.8	5.8	6.7	6.6	5.9	5.0	5.7	5.4	5.2	4.6	3.6
Soccer	41.3	38.5	38.3	35.1	29.7	26.8	18.7	16.4	16.4	12.5	8.2	4.6	2.8
Softball	70.9	69.2	72.5	72.5	69.6	68.4	65.6	65.6	67.1	65.6	62.3	58.9	48.4
Squash	3.6	3.6	3.2	3.0	3.4	3.3	2.0	2.0	2.9	2.7	2.8	2.5	2.3
Swimming/diving	53.6	53.3	55.0	54.9	54.2	53.5	44.8	42.5	49.1	48.6	46.9	44.8	41.0
Synchronized swimming	0.5	0.5	0.7	0.7	1.5	1.3	1.5	1.3	2.7	3.3	3.2	3.4	3.3
Tennis	88.8	88.8	88.9	90.3	88.5	87.0	82.5	82.6	85.5	85.4	88.6	86.5	80.0
Track and field	68.6	66.8	66.8	64.4	67.2	63.8	58.7	57.2	62.0	59.3	58.6	54.3	46.1
Volleyball	90.6	91.2	91.2	91.0	87.7	86.3	84.0	83.6	85.7	84.9	87.8	85.9	80.1

PERCENTAGE OF FEMALE COACHES OF WOMEN'S TEAMS, ALL DIVISIONS

1994	49.4
1993	48.1
1992	48.3
1991	47.7
1990	47.3
1989	47.7
1988	48.3
1987	48.8
1986	50.6
1985	50.7
1984	53.8
1983	56.2
1982	52.4
1981	54.6
1980	54.2
1979	56.1
1978	58.2

PERCENTAGE OF FEMALE COACHES OF WOMEN'S TEAMS, BY DIVISION

	DIVISION 1	DIVISION 2	DIVISION 3
1994	46.9	45.4	53.6
1993	45.5	44.1	52.3
1992	46.6	42.3	52.6
1991	45.9	42.1	51.7
1990	44.2	44.0	51.8
1988	43.8	45.7	53.3
1986	45.5	46.8	57.2
1984	49.9	52.2	58.8

PERCENTAGE OF FEMALE COACHES OF WOMEN'S TEAMS, 1978–1990, ALL DIVISIONS

	1990	1989	1988	1987	1986	1985	1984	1983	1982	1981	1980	1979	1978
Archery	80.0	80.0	66.6	71.4	60.0	80.0	77.7	83.3	58.3	60.0	76.5	75.0	83.4
Badminton	50.0	33.3	66.7	71.4	66.6	75.0	57.1	62.5	70.8	72.4	72.7	73.0	75.0
Basketball	59.9	60.0	58.5	59.9	61.0	62.7	64.9	66.6	71.2	73.7	76.5	77.7	79.4
Bowling	0.0	0.0	11.1	9.1	16.7	16.7	28.6	35.7	47.4	45.5	40.9	36.4	42.9
Crew/rowing	39.1	34.9	27.0	21.0	22.0	29.1	23.5	26.9	26.6	29.4	18.2	19.1	11.9
Cross country	20.6	20.0	19.5	18.7	21.8	21.1	19.7	22.4	21.6	22.0	25.0	29.9	35.2
Fencing	28.9	28.9	30.8	33.3	32.7	35.2	37.2	40.7	34.7	35.4	37.3	46.6	51.7
Field hockey	97.8	97.3	96.2	96.8	97.1	93.8	98.2	96.2	99.6	98.3	98.3	97.4	99.1
Golf	41.1	45.4	41.3	37.5	44.1	37.5	39.7	40.4	48.9	49.6	46.3	55.1	54.6
Gymnastics	57.5	59.8	53.7	55.6	55.7	55.4	59.1	60.1	67.3	68.7	66.6	68.0	69.7
Ice hockey	12.5	0.0	0.0	0.0	46.7	37.5	9.5	11.1	21.1	26.4	18.2	11.1	37.5
Lacrosse	95.1	94.2	95.2	95.1	89.0	90.1	95.0	93.9	96.9	96.7	100.0	100.0	90.7
Riding/equestrian	85.7	85.7	100.0	100.0	81.2	78.6	89.5	94.4	93.8	93.4	73.7	73.4	75.0
Riflery	12.5	18.3	13.3	5.6	16.0	12.0	4.8	0.0	0.0	7.7	19.0	10.0	17.4
Sailing	12.5	4.3	5.3	5.6	5.9	6.2	15.0	19.0	22.2	31.3	8.3	13.3	7.1
Skiing	21.9	18.8	18.2	15.2	48.6	7.7	13.8	13.5	15.8	16.7	25.0	25.0	22.7
Soccer	23.1	23.9	23.0	24.1	30.7	23.9	26.8	30.6	33.0	27.7	28.0	35.7	29.4
Softball	63.8	64.6	67.2	67.5	68.0	64.9	68.6	70.9	74.6	75.8	82.9	83.1	83.5
Squash	68.2	72.1	66.7	70.6	60.0	50.0	40.0	53.3	63.2	61.2	53.0	73.3	71.4
Swimming/diving	26.4	24.4	26.3	25.7	30.0	31.2	33.2	35.0	36.5	41.4	44.8	50.9	53.6
Synchronized swimming	100.0	100.0	100.0	100.0	100.0	100.0	72.7	90.0	100.0	95.3	95.0	90.0	85.0
Tennis	49.8	52.2	52.2	54.9	54.8	56.9	59.7	61.5	65.3	66.1	68.9	71.6	72.9
Track and field	19.6	21.6	21.6	20.8	23.1	24.1	26.8	30.6	33.7	34.8	43.1	46.5	52.3
Volleyball	68.4	71.0	71.0	70.2	71.3	72.0	75.5	76.7	74.8	78.0	83.7	83.6	86.6

PERCENTAGE OF FEMALE ATHLETIC DIRECTORS FOR WOMEN'S INTERCOLLEGIATE ATHLETIC PROGRAMS

1994	21.0
1992	16.8
1990	15.9
1988	16.1
1986	15.2
1984	17.0
1980	20.0
1972	90+

PERCENTAGE OF ATHLETIC PROGRAMS TOTALLY LACKING ANY FEMALE ADMINISTRATOR, BY DIVISION

YEAR	DIVISION 1	DIVISION 2	DIVISION 3
1994	9.9	44.7	21.5
1992	14.6	38.8	31.9
1990	21.8	39.9	32.8
1988	25.6	33.3	37.0
1986	23.4	34.1	38.3
1984	21.4	36.9	36.9

ADMINISTRATIVE JOBS ABSOLUTE NUMBER

YEAR	ALL SCHOOLS	MALE	FEMALE	PERCENT FEMALE
1992	2,286	1,580	704	30.8
1990	1,874	1,274	600	32.0
1988	1,827	1,299	528	28.9
1986	1,613			

PERCENTAGE OF ATHLETIC PROGRAMS TOTALLY LACKING ANY FEMALE ADMINISTRATOR, ALL DIVISIONS*

1994	24.4
1992	27.8
1990	30.3
1988	32.5
1986	31.9
1984	31.6

*These programs lack *any* females *anywhere* in the administrative structure. This means there are *no* assistant and *no* associate female athletic directors and the head athletic director is a male.

When Title IX was enacted June 23, 1972, over 90% of women's intercollegiate athletics programs were administered by a female while almost no females administered men's teams. Most of the female AD's had their roots in physical education and often continued to teach while serving as the AD of a large but basically underfunded women's athletic program.

Many of the female athletic directors in the 1970s also coached a team or two. As daunting as their workload was, it is important to recall that the length of the competitive season was much shorter at the time Title IX was enacted.

* * *

Three main reasons existed for such short seasons:

1. Lack of funding

2. Society's former and persistent belief that females lacked the stamina to endure a competitive season as vigorous as their male counterparts

3. Coaches were generally volunteering their time and they had finite hours to devote to coaching while also carrying out full-time teaching loads.

JESSICA GAVORA

How Women Beat Men at College Sports, 1995

In the early 1990s, colleges and universities, propelled by court decisions and by the demands of their undergraduates, began to add women's sports at a significant rate. In response, a new set of critics of Title IX emerged. Jessica Gavora was one of the first of these new critics of the law. Occupying a privileged position as a female who was arguing that the law discriminated against males, she laid out an influential critique echoed by many others.

The article reprinted here, one of her early writings, lays out some of the questions that are central to the game. Is Title IX the same as Affirmative Action and, if so, is that morally objectionable? Do women actually want to participate in sports at the same rate as men? If not, should universities be freed from any obligation to provide them the same opportunities? And are efforts to add opportunities actually privileging white women while leaving African American and Latinx women behind?

As you read, recognize that this is an op-ed piece, without the space to provide extensive evidence to support Gavora's argument. Advocates for Title IX will argue that Gavora misreads this evidence. During the game, you will have to do additional research to provide support for your claims.

*Finally, the court case Gavora refers to (Cohen v. Brown) was appealed short-
ly after the district court decision. This appeal has not yet been ruled upon. You
may not cite any material from that case after the district court decision.*

SOURCE: *Jessica Gavora, "How Women Beat Men at College Sports,"* Women's Quarterly 5 (1995): 4–5.

For critics of identity politics, there was a measure of justice in a scene played out before a congressional committee last spring. Vartan Gregorian, the president of Brown University, was still smarting from a U.S. district court ruling against Brown in a sex bias case. He complained bitterly to the committee—which was reviewing sex discrimination in school sports—of the "assault against common sense" the court had perpetrated, with the aid of federal authorities, in the name of "gender equity" on his campus.

Brown stood accused of violating federal law because its female students participate in sports at lesser rates than its male students. The court had judged this as evidence of discrimination. Gregorian, no enemy of political correctness, was there to tell the congressmen that things had finally gone too far. Like a scene from a bad science fiction movie, the creature created in the laboratory of liberalism had mutated into something wild and uncontrollable, and this mad scientist was not liking it one bit.

College sports are required—by Title IX of the 1972 education amendments to the Civil Rights Act of 1964—to provide equal opportunities for men and women. Although enacted as an anti-discrimination statute, Title IX has quietly become a quota system that has decreased sports opportunities for men while demanding endlessly expanding opportunities for women. What's more, the losers from Title IX are not limited to the now familiar angry white male. Pursuit of "gender equity" in college athletics is alienating key parts of the affirmative action constituency—black males and liberal college administrators—while minority women see little benefit. The only clear winners, for the time being, are middle-and upper-class white women.

Because men tend to participate in sports at higher rates than women, university administrators—under pressure both to comply with Title IX and balance their budgets—resort to simply cutting men's athletic slots to avoid the charge that women are "under-represented" in sports. But when men's opportunities are cut in sports such as basketball and football—which have high concentrations of minority athletes—"gender equity" often supplants racial equity, spelling trouble in the world of race and sex bean-counting. Last year, the National Collegiate Athletic Association (NCAA) voted to cut men's basketball scholarships while leaving women's untouched, raising howls of protest from black coaches. At many universities, non-scholarship slots on large men's basketball, football, and track squads are being trimmed—taking opportunities for black male athletes with them. At some schools, these sports are being eliminated altogether.

And who benefits? The women's teams most often added to achieve Title IX compliance are in sports like tennis, rowing, and soccer—not the stuff of heated competition in the inner city. NCAA statistics bear this out: The women who participate in these sports (that is, sports other than women's basketball and track) are eighty-six percent white, five percent black and two percent Hispanic.

Women's participation in college sports has exploded since Title IX was enacted in 1972, rising from fewer than ten percent of coeds to almost forty percent today. Since 1982, the NCAA reports that 366 schools have started women's soccer teams, while ninety-nine have discontinued men's wrestling and sixty-four have eliminated men's swimming. Men's gymnastics is on the verge of extinction at the college level, having gone from 133 teams in 1975 to thirty-two today. Meanwhile, women's tennis has soared from twenty-two Division I squads in 1982 to 131 today. The anecdotal evidence is equally revealing. Notre Dame, which eliminated men's wrestling in 1991, and may drop hockey this year, cannot afford to offer its male lacrosse players scholarship assistance—never mind that they were one of the four best teams in the nation last year. The university, meanwhile, just decided to add two new women's sports.

Athough Title IX has been on the books for more than twenty years, it did not blossom as an enforcer of quota systems until the Clinton administration. The number of "compliance reviews" (that is, investigations undertaken without any formal complaint of discrimination) by the Department of Education Office of Civil Rights (OCR) increased more than fourfold in the first year of Clinton's presidency. That same year, Title IX complaints doubled as plaintiffs sensed a more receptive federal audience. Each of these complaints was investigated by the OCR, which holds the trump card of ending federal funding if targeted institutions do not agree to toe the line.

Theoretically, the OCR uses three tests to determine compliance: proportionality; seeing that the athletic "interests and abilities" of women on campus have been satisfied; or by observing a history of increasing sports opportunities for women. Colleges, the OCR contends, need only meet one of these tests to get a clean bill of health. Such is the theory. Brown had drawn rave reviews from proponents and critics of Title IX alike for having a model program in women's sports. Still, when university administrators, desperate for cash, had the temerity to try to downgrade two women's sports from varsity to club status, female athletes sued and an epic legal battle followed. Brown lost. As Gregorian noted, the regulations are so elastic that schools are left in the position of continuously improving women's sports opportunities, regardless of interest or need—or face a lawsuit. "I cannot tell these women, 'You better participate in athletics otherwise you cause problems,' " he complained.

Discontent has not been limited to Brown. The president of Eastern Illinois University testified that a "voluntary" Title IX compliance agreement forced the university to cut two men's sports in order to add four for women. One of the programs foisted on EIU was women's field hockey, a sport, the university complained, that is not even played in Illinois. Willie Myers, the athletic director at the University of Wisconsin-Whitewater, described a recent Title IX compliance review by federal officials as "the most frustrating and stressful [experience] that I have ever encountered in my professional career."

Despite repeated pleas from coaches and administrators for clearer rules, Clinton OCR head Norma Cantu testified before Congress that issuing more definitive regulations would make Title IX "prescriptive and inflexible." In fact, the Clinton OCR has a history of relying on vague, open-ended regulations to achieve its ends. Experience has taught Clinton administration educrats that the threat of federal investigation and messy lawsuits is more effective—and easier to wield—than traditional legal or regulatory means.

Under pressure from Congress, which has threatened to end federal enforcement of "gender equity" on campus unless more objective criteria for Title IX compliance are issued, Cantu has promised to clarify the guidelines. A Department of Education source, however, said what is likely to emerge—if anything—is another issuance of "interpretation of the existing policy interpretation." In other words, not real regulatory relief but a redrawn blueprint for continued bureaucratic activism.

U.S. CONGRESS

Hearing on Title IX of the Education Amendments of 1972

The U.S. Congress held hearings on Title IX in March (the House) and October (the Senate) of 1995. These hearings were short and ended without any changes to the law or its implementation.

However, advocates for and against amending Title IX or altering its enforcement criteria used the hearings to vent their frustrations and defend their own positions. As a result, the records of the hearing offer an invaluable window into the debate.

Every player will find something of use here. Advocates of men's Olympic ("minor") sports will want to pay careful attention to the statements of Hastert and Kerr. Supporters of football will benefit from a careful reading of the statement of Charles Neinas. And defenders of Title IX will find much support in the arguments made by Cardiss Collins and Wendy Hilliard.

Most of the major figures in these hearings submitted extensive reports containing evidence for their statements. These reports are not included here. However, an ambitious player will benefit from finding these reports and using the data they provide.

Some short passages have been cut for length and coherence.

SOURCE: *Hearing before the Subcommittee on Postsecondary Education, Training, and Life-long Learning of the Committee on Economic and Educational Opportunities, House of Representatives, One Hundred Fourth Congress, first session, hearing held in Washington, DC, May 9, 1995.*

PREPARED STATEMENT OF J. DENNIS HASTERT, MEMBER OF CONGRESS (IL-14) BEFORE THE SUBCOMMITTEE ON POSTSECONDARY EDUCATION, TRAINING AND LIFELONG LEARNING

May 9, 1995

*M*r. Chairman, I very much appreciate the opportunity to speak this morning and I thank you for your interest and help in holding this hearing.

My interest in the issues surrounding Title IX of the Educational Amendments of 1972 has been fostered in many ways. First, I am a former wrestler and I coached wrestling for 16 years at Yorkville High School, my home town. I love this sport and the kids I coached. I was President of the Illinois Wrestling Coach's Association in 1975 and 1976 and came out to Washington several times to lobby on the Amateur Sports Act.

Secondly, I recently began receiving hundreds of letters from youngsters around the nation who are no longer able to participate in sports because their sport is being eliminated at their various university. I have heard from kids from California all the way to Pennsylvania. They don't understand how a school can promise them the opportunity to compete and drop the program half way through their eligibility.

Also, coaches representing a wide variety of sports, including wrestling, gymnastics, track and field, rowing, baseball, swimming, soccer, water sports, volleyball and fencing have created a coalition to halt this alarming trend. I would like to take a moment to introduce a very distinguished coach and Olympian who is sitting in the audience today. Dan Gable is somewhat of a legend in wrestling. He won the world championship in 1971 at the age of 22, the youngest American ever to do so at that time. The next year he won the gold medal at the 1972 Olympics in Munich without surrendering even a single point! Dan is here today because he is very concerned about the trend we see out there. The oldest sport known to man is disappearing faster than any supposed "lack of interest" could possibly explain.

It was not hard to notice this trend getting out of hand in my own state. Western Illinois University dropped its wrestling program a couple years ago. The

University of Illinois dropped its men's swim team resulting in a lawsuit alleging reverse discrimination. Northern Illinois University, in my own Congressional District, proposed to eliminate wrestling and swimming last fall. Eastern Illinois University followed closely behind with an announcement to drop wrestling and swimming. President David Jorns from Eastern is here today to tell you about their experience. Most recently, Illinois State University has announced its intention to eliminate wrestling and soccer. This is just in the state of Illinois in the last few years! But it's happening all across the United States.

When these sports are eliminated, the universities cite their need to comply with Title IX and the proportionality rule as part or all of their reason. *While I want all schools to comply with Title IX, I strongly believe that the elimination of opportunities was not the intent of Title IX.* These lost opportunities are what I call the "unintended consequences" of Title IX.

So, why would a university cut sports to comply with Title IX? Title IX was supposed to be a statute to increase opportunities.

Let me explain briefly. One way a university tries to comply with Title IX is by meeting the "opportunities test." That is, effectively accommodating the interests and abilities of both genders. There are numerous tests (13) that a school must meet in order to comply with Title IX and ensure there is no discrimination in their athletic programs. These range from money spent on scholarships to coach's salaries to athletic facilities. However, it is the opportunities test that forces schools to drop certain sports. The opportunities test is made up of three parts: 1) the proportionality rule, which says the participation opportunities of male and female students must be in numbers substantially proportionate to their respective enrollment rates, 2) the history and continuing practice of program expansion for the underrepresented sex, and 3) the accommodation of the athletic interests and abilities of the underrepresented sex. According to the Office of Civil Rights of the Department of Education (OCR), meeting any one of these factors signals compliance.

However, that is not what I have been hearing from the field, and the courts have *de facto* made proportionality the only applicable standard. It is interesting to note that the original statute states only the following:

> No person in the United States shall, on the basis of sex, be excluded from participation in, be denied the benefits of, or be subjected to discrimination under any education program or activity receiving financial assistance.

This language does not mandate a proportionality rule. Proportionality comes out of the 1979 Policy Interpretation developed by the Department of Education. However, the courts have given proportionality preference.

The second and third prongs of the opportunities test have largely lost all meaning in terms of compliance. For instance, a school which made improvements by adding numerous new teams for female athletes soon after Title IX first became law may no longer be considered to be in compliance unless they are now planning to add new sports. When can they stop adding new sports for anyone interested? Well, when they have met the proportionality test.

The third prong is even more nebulous than the first. How is the concept of "interests and abilities" measured? It is entirely unclear whether the university can take surveys and use them as representations of the interests and abilities of the student population due to recent court decisions. Some will claim that surveys can not show the latent interest that would be there if a sport were offered. How in the world is a university to comply with a standard like that?! Thus, schools fall back on, you guessed it, the proportionality rule.

So, if a university's numbers do not add up—they either add opportunities for women (which is in line with providing more opportunities as Congress intended), or they eliminate enough men's sports teams to meet their numerical objectives (what I consider to be the opposite of Congressional intent).

The proportionality rule is easier—because universities know what they have to do to comply. No one is sure how to comply with interests and abilities nor does OCR give universities much direction on these issues.

In fact, in some cases, it appears OCH actually makes it seem that there is no way to comply with Title IX unless a university reaches proportionality. Again and again, universities submit plans to OCR for compliance, only to have them rejected because they do not attain substantial proportionality.

This *de facto* reliance on proportionality alone leads me to these questions: Are we as a nation saying that numbers alone indicate discrimination? Has this, in fact, become a quota system? And more importantly, have we created a quota system that does not help the underrepresented sex as much as it should because universities simply cut the "overrepresented" sex as a means of meeting the test? It does not help create opportunities for women when a school simply cuts a sport such as soccer, swimming or wrestling to comply.

And we should not support such tactics. This only hurts young women and men across the nation who are denied the opportunities that should be afforded to them.

The benefits of sport in general—the values of fair play and teamwork, of stretching yourself to the fullest and pushing your body to its utmost performance—will be lost on these women and men who will not get the opportunity they should have. They are caught in the unintended consequences of Title IX. They are caught in a quota system which makes them a number and not an athlete. It is not what Congress intended and it should not be allowed to continue.

Many claim the problem is money. But even this argument rings hollow when you consider the investigators manual does not exempt teams supported by private funds (using no federal money) from the proportionality equation. For instance, at Princeton University, the Wrestling Alumni put forward a $2.3 million endowment for the $100,000 per year program. But this does not keep Princeton from having to comply with proportionality rules.

So, what are the answers to this dilemma? I do not claim to have all of the answers today, and I am as anxious as you are to hear the testimony of so many who are struggling with this issue. They are really the experts. However, I would like to offer some thoughts on where Congress should be headed.

The overriding goals should be to follow policies that encourage schools to add, rather than subtract athletic opportunity.

As I alluded to earlier, OCR should give more specific guidance to universities about how they can comply with the second and third prongs of the "opportunities test." Congress should take back control of this process because the courts are making determinations that bring everything back to proportionality.

OCH then, in turn, acquiesces to court rulings. The second and third prongs become meaningless if they are not further defined. Congress has abrogated our responsibility if we allow this to continue.

OCR also needs to clearly define who is a participant for the purposes of those calculations. Should a school count every kid who tries out for the team, everyone who suited up for competition, or should opportunity slots be counted? For instance, should a school count a cross country runner who also runs track as one participant or two athletic opportunity slots? And, should universities be held responsible if the slots they have open for women are then not filled? These issues are also part of an ongoing rulemaking in response to Equity in Athletics Disclosure Act passed by Congress last year. These issues are important to any university that seeks to comply with the proportionality test.

However, maybe we need to think in broader terms—to find a way to encourage Title IX compliance without the use of quotas. We do not assume that everyone who enrolls at a university wants (or given the opportunity would) be in band. Let's face it, not everyone wants to play the tuba. But we operate under similar assumptions when we consider athletics. Proportionality, at the very least should be based on those in the interested population rather than everyone. I urge the committee to consider creative solutions to ending the continuing discrimination out there without using proportionality.

Finally, I challenge all of us to think about our intent in this legislation. Did Congress intend for Title IX to result in the elimination of athletic opportunities for anyone? Can any of us say that we want Title IX to be implemented in such a way?

It really disturbs me when people claims that it is fine to cut opportunities for men to eradicate discrimination. Well, Mr. Chairman—that is not fine. That view represents everything that is wrong about Title IX. When it ceases to be a law to work for positive improvements in the future and simply becomes a way to get back at the systems that perpetrated discrimination, we have lost our focus of what it means to work toward gender equity. It doesn't help anyone to just keep tearing the future of these kids out from under them.

So, I hope this hearing will lay the groundwork for some positive changes to our present system of Title IX. Thank you for your attention.

PREPARED TESTIMONY OF HON. CARDISS COLLINS BEFORE SUBCOMMITTEE ON POST SECONDARY EDUCATION, TRAINING, AND LIFE-LONG LEARNING

May 9, 1995

Mr. Chairman, and Members of the subcommittee, I appreciate this opportunity to testify on Title IX and its impact upon sports. For the past four years, when I chaired the Subcommittee on Commerce, Consumer Protection, and Competitiveness, I took a particular interest in this subject. The Subcommittee held four hearings on gender equity, and four others on college sports general, conducted workshops, attended NCAA meetings, and had the opportunity to listen to dozens of interested parties in the subject.

During that period, I learned that many concepts taken as facts simply are not. Frankly, I have learned that there is only one overriding fact, and it is simply this:

The number of girls and young women interested in participating in sports has been increasing in leaps and bounds over the past two decades.

That's a very simple truth, but it is at the heart of the debate over Title IX, and one that cannot be ignored. Too often those with very little contact with what is going on in our schools, or perhaps those without daughters, fail to understand the sports scene is radically different from [how] it was a generation ago. Vast numbers of girls and young women are now playing sports with the same enthusiasm that generations of boys and young men have shown. They play all kinds of sports, and they play them well.

Whether Title IX has been responsible for generating this enthusiasm, or instead, has been a force to make schools react to this interest is irrelevant. What is relevant is that women want the same opportunities as men, and Title IX guarantees them that right.

I am sure that during the course of your hearings you will hear the same arguments that you hear against affirmative action—namely that Title IX is taking opportunities away from men, or that Title IX establishes quotas for women. Most of these arguments come from school administrators or football coaches who fear that increasing opportunities for women will come out of their hides.

The reality is the exact opposite. Athletic directors and coaches are the ones who establish quotas at the schools. They decide, often arbitrarily, how many men and how many women get to play sports. Schools, not the Department of Education, are responsible for quotas assuring that men receive over two-thirds of all opportunities, and 75 cents out of every dollar spent on sports. The purpose of

Title IX is to eliminate these artificial quotas, and permit opportunities to be based upon student interest, without gender bias.

Title IX simply says that no person shall, on the basis of sex, be excluded from participation in, be denied the benefits of, or be subjected to discrimination under any education program or activity receiving Federal financial assistance.

The law does not require fixed quotas. The law has been interpreted to mean that if schools have participation rates equal to enrollment rates, the school is automatically considered in compliance. However, even if the numbers are not the same, the regulations allow a school to show compliance either through a history of expanding opportunities in women's programs, or by showing that the interests of women have been fully accommodated.

This is not an odd interpretation of the law. The NCAA Gender Equity Task Force Report of July 26, 1993 states, "The ultimate goal for each institution should be that the numbers of male and female athletes are substantially proportionate to their numbers in [the] institution's undergraduate student population." The report continues, "Thus, the (a) participation, (b) efforts and (c) interests tests of the Title IX regulation are the appropriate tests for equitable participation." The report also notes that "proportionality does not require fixed quotas."

Unfortunately, some school administrators have been opposed to these simple guidelines, which were endorsed by the NCAA. In some cases, they have dismal records of participation of women, show no efforts to increase opportunities for women, and in the face of protests over the cutting of women's team sports, go into court with a straight face and argue that there just isn't interest by women in sports. Their arguments often have as much foundation as Al Campanis's assertion that Blacks lack the skills to be major league managers.

To understand what Title IX is all about, let me just provide two analogies. Suppose a family has a son and he enjoys playing ball in the backyard, basketball at the gym, or soccer at the park. A second child comes along, but the family income does not change. Do we assume that the second child's interests in the same sports can only be accommodated at the expense of the first child? Of course not. It may become necessary for the two children to learn to share the baseball bat or the basketball. We don't give one child some artificial priority over supplies, or even the use of the back yard. You would be surprised that many of the Title IX cases boil down to little more than the need for the men's teams to share resources, share playing fields, and share prime times with the women's teams.

Let's look at an analogy in the schools. Suppose that women take an increasing interest in chemistry, and start enrolling in greater numbers for chemistry courses. The school may do a number of things to accommodate this increased interest. They may add more teachers, establish additional lab times, build more labs, or create bigger classes. It is also possible that some kids may just not be able to take the class, as often happens at colleges when popular courses are oversubscribed. The one policy that I think we all recognize is unthinkable, however, would be a policy that says we will accommodate the additional interest by women only after the traditional number of male students is accommodated. The same should be true for sports.

Observers of college sports can recount dozens of examples of patterns of sex discrimination over decades. Women often have far inferior training facilities, practice fields, practice times and game times. On road trips there may be three or four women to a room, while the men have single rooms. In the case of Colgate, where the women's team wanted to increase their budget from $6,000 to $12,000, but were denied, the school increased the men's team's *stick budget* to the same $12,000. The men's team had a budget of $300,000, while the women received $4,000

At the start of my testimony I mentioned that the biggest problem in the debate over Title IX is the assumption of "facts" that are actually myths. Therefore, let me leave you with just a few of these myths, and the actual facts.

Myth#1: The increased participation of women in sports has come at the expense of men. The facts: According to the NCAA, over the past 15 years, participation in women's sports increased by 16,320 while participation in men's sports increased by 12,320. For every new dollar spent on women, $2 have been spent on men.

Myth #2: Football actually pays the cost of women's sports, so football should be excluded from Title IX considerations. The facts: According to the NCAA, an analysis of 1989 budgets found that 45% of Division I-A schools reported a deficit in football, while 94% of Division I-AA reported a deficit. Of Divisions II and III schools, 93% operated at a deficit. Of the 45% of Division 1-A schools reporting a deficit in football, the average deficit was $638,000, which was up from $251,000 in 1981.

Myth #3: The Department of Education is imposing quotas on schools for Title IX compliance. The facts: The Department of Education and the Office of Civil Rights have been spectacularly unsuccessful in forcing schools to do anything. A study by the LBJ School of Public Affairs at the University of Texas found that "OCR has failed to provide effective and adequate enforcement and guidance consistent with the letter and spirit of Title IX." In fact, victims of sex discrimination testified at our hearings that OCR was the last place they would go to seek relief. They turned to the courts.

Myth #4: Women's sports have no popularity with the public, and therefore can generate no revenue. The facts: While it is true that schools that fail to provide any promotion for women's sports and schedule games at odd hours find the results self-fulfilling, interest in women's sports is on the rise. At Stanford, average attendance for women's basketball was 5,284 compared to 5,386 for the men. The 17,000 seats for the women's Final Four games were sold out last September. The women's final game on Sunday afternoon had higher ratings than the NBA game opposite it, and higher ratings than a men's semifinal the day before.

In summary, when you get to know the facts, you find out that the issue is simply how do schools accommodate the growing interest in women's sports. If schools stick to quotas to ensure an artificial advantage for men, the courts will strike them down. However, if schools take steps to accommodate this interest, everyone's child will benefit. It is time for schools to share their resources fairly, and eliminate their self-imposed quotas.

THE COMMITTEE DISCUSSION WITH HASTERT, COLLINS, AND OTHERS

Chairman McKEON. Thank you. We have some Members here today who are not on our subcommittee, and we appreciate their interest. We have Representative Ganske from Iowa; Bill Barrett from Nebraska who is on our full committee, but is not a Member of this subcommittee; Mrs. Mink from Hawaii; and Ranking Member of the full committee Mr. Shaw from Missouri.

We will try to hold the questions to the Members of the committee unless you have—

Mr. CLAY. Chairman, don't confuse me with Clay Shaw.

Mr. WILLIAMS. This is William Clay.

Chairman McKEON. Actually, Clay Shaw is a great one to be confused with, and I apologize.

Mr. CLAY. He is a good friend of mine, too.

Chairman McKEON. But it is nice to be recognized for who we really are. And again, I am new at this and appreciate your forbearance.

Mr. Williams, are you ready for questions?

Mr. WILLIAMS. Thank you, Mr. Chairman.

Congressman, much of your testimony with regard to the fix that you would like to see enacted for Title IX had to do with rulemaking. Are you encouraging a legislative change that would require a change in rulemaking?

Mr. HASTERT. Well, I think the law certainly set out a policy that, over the years, has been developed by the Department of Education, now OCR, and I think is misdirected. I think the proportionality rule is something of "unintended consequences." It was never intended to cut back participation of men in athletics. I mean, this is the only civil rights law that I know of that punishes innocent bystanders, and this is what is happening at many of our universities today.

I can give you numbers of sports that have been diminished in the last decade. But what I am saying is that we need to take a look at the use of proportionality. There is a three pronged rule. Proportionality is one. Accommodating interests and abilities is another. Showing a history and continuing practice of program expansion in the past three years is the other prong. You know the original rulemaking said all three prongs should be treated in an equal way—that is, complying with any one of the three meets the standards. That is not being done today. Proportionality is the only one that is being considered.

Mr. WILLIAMS. But that is all an interest of rulemaking rather than the law. That is not in the law. Those are in the regulations. Would you have us require a change in the rulemaking process?

Mr. HASTERT. As you see, I don't have legislation, but this needs to be brought forward. We need to look at it. That is one of the jobs of Congress, to have oversight on what is happening. And I think we need to elevate that and take a look at it because I don't think that was the intent of the law and that is exactly why we are doing it.

Mr. WILLIAMS. Thank you.

Congresswoman Collins, we appreciate the good work that you and your committee have done in previous Congresses concerning oversight of this matter. Did you find any "unintended consequences" from Title IX during your oversight visits or hearings?

Mrs. COLLINS. No, I did not find any "unintended consequences" at all of the law itself. What I did find was a reluctance on the part of school administrators to fully implement Title IX. When Title IX first became law, a great number of universities began to comply. As time went on, that interest began to fade. By the time we looked at the law again, we found very little compliance at all. What had happened is that somebody had just forgotten that Title IX was on the books, and they weren't doing anything about it.

What surprised me the most during our hearings and investigations was the fact that, even though Title IX was on the books, OCR was not as vigilant as it could have been. What has happened as of now is that instead of OCR looking at this and saying, well, Federal dollars are not being spent fairly, they sort of closed their eyes to that and left an opening for young students themselves to look into Title IX and take their cases to court themselves.

Now it seems to me that is an awful burden to put on a student—to have to go through the judicial system on their own to say, well, we want to play soccer. We, as girls, have a right to be engaged in sports, as do boys in whatever their activities happen to be.

It has been reported here, and many people seem to think, that there has been a decline in men's sports, but there has been, on the other hand, sort of a seesaw effect, if you will, where there has been a decline in men's sports, there has been an increase in women's sports, so the things are beginning to balance out because of the renewed interest in Title IX.

The one thing I do want to point out is this and everybody—both Congressman Hastert and I haven't really focused on the big point. The big point around Title IX happens to center around money. Football, it seems to me, is thought to be sacrosanct in our colleges and universities. That is because college football—to a large degree because of the advent of television and televised football games—is a big money maker. It isn't the only money maker for a college or university, but it is the one that the coaches and athletes and the Presidents want to keep.

Because of that, everybody says, well, you know, we can get rid of wrestling. We can get rid of men in other activities, but we are going to keep the football team, and we are going to have squads of a hundred on the football team—twice as many as we have for the Chicago Bears, as a matter of fact—and we are going to give them all this money. We are going to have them traveling the country in airplanes and roaring up the road in air-conditioned buses, whereas the women are not going to have these kinds of funds. The men are going to have their own rooms when they play out of their school environment. Women are going to have three or four in one room. They are not going to have the same kind of practice time. They are not going to have the soccer fields. They are not going to have many of the things that are provided for the young men. This is nefarious, something that has to be corrected.

Title IX hopes to correct some of these problems. It seems to me we have to talk about the whole thing. The one thing that seems to be forgotten—and then I am going to conclude—is that the primary function of any educational institution is to educate our children, to teach them goals and morals and high standards, et cetera. But when we have discrimination involved, one group of people against another, women against men, we are not doing our jobs. There is more than teaching literature. There is more than teaching theatrics. There are other things that are life enhancing, and certainly the ability to participate in a fair manner in an educational institution is something we want our girls to know as well as men.

Mr. WILLIAMS. Thank you, Mrs. Collins. Mr. Chairman, . . .

Chairman McKEON. Mr. Funderburk.

Mr. FUNDERBURK. No questions, Mr. Chairman.

Chairman McKEON. Mr. Gunderson.

Mr. GUNDERSON. Thank you, Mr. Chairman.

I had three 9 a.m. meetings, so I apologize for being late. I want to follow up, Congresswoman Collins, on your comments there. I assume—and I mean this in a positive sense—you are a supporter of affirmative action.

Mrs. COLLINS. All the way.

Mr. GUNDERSON. I am not sure, I am struggling with that one myself. But isn't the premise of affirmative action to take where we are and to build upon that? My concern with the interpretation of Title IX is that it doesn't build up women's sports.

Mrs. COLLINS. But it has.

Mr. GUNDERSON. Does it say that we are going to bring men down to have an equal level? I don't know how we get there from here.

Mrs. COLLINS. It doesn't bring men down. It hasn't brought men down. What has happened is that in order to make a point and to keep from lowering the number of men on these huge football squads, these athletic directors and coaches have decided to sacrifice the men who happen to be in gymnastics, those who happen to be in soccer, those who happen to be on swimming teams, et cetera, so the students will be the ones who are saying, you know, we have been treated unfairly.

This has happened in our State, as Mr. Hastert has pointed out, and it has happened across the country. The fair thing to say is, well, you don't need 100 young men on a football squad. You need so many men to play football but you also need women because women are interested in sports. They like teamwork. They need to know how to be competitive. They want to feel good about themselves in a sports arena as well as men. That is the thing about fairness. That is about the whole boat rising up, if you will.

Mr. GUNDERSON. I am not against—

Mrs. COLLINS. And I—

Mr. GUNDERSON. [continuing] against sports in any way, shape, or form. My question is: Is the only way to achieve that by tearing down men's sports?

Mrs. COLLINS. I don't think they are being torn down.

Mr. GUNDERSON. How are you going to finance all of this?

Mrs. COLLINS. How is it being financed now?

Mr. GUNDERSON. Not out of the Federal budget.

Mrs. COLLINS. Are you saying that the funds that the Federal Government gives to these colleges and universities should all go to the men and not go to the women? I don't think that is what is intended.

Mr. GUNDERSON. Frankly, I don't think any taxpayer dollars ought to go to sports.

Mrs. COLLINS. Why?

Mr. GUNDERSON. Because I think there are higher priorities in American society than for taxpayer dollars to go to college sports.

Mrs. COLLINS. Well, if that is what you want—let's in fact make sure that Title IX is spent exactly as you want it to be spent and that is when a college or university does not comply with Title IX they should not get any more Federal funds. That is what Title IX—

Mr. GUNDERSON. That is what I understand.

Mr. Hastert wants to comment.

Mr. HASTERT. My good friend and colleague, and we have worked on a lot of issues together in a more amicable way, the fact is that in the State of Illinois, you know, it wasn't the administration that cut the sports on many of those issues, it was the OCR that said you had to cut a minor sport. They didn't say you had to cut football. They said you cut swimming. You cut soccer. You cut baseball. Cut wrestling. That is exactly what happened, and those schools were given that choice and only that choice to meet proportionality.

I can tell you, I disagree with my friend from Illinois. For example, in men's gymnastics, 20 years ago, when we had the 1976 Olympics, we had 138 teams competing in gymnastics—a very successful year at the Montreal Olympics. Today, only 31 teams are competing in gymnastics in this Nation. Thirty-one teams is not enough teams to have a national tournament. That means future generations of young men will be deprived of coaches to further their ability to participate in this one sport.

Wrestling, men's swimming, and water polo have all had divisions in danger of losing their championships. Wrestling lost 120 programs in the last 10 years. One hundred twenty programs, Congresswoman.

Mrs. COLLINS. Did those programs go to the women?

Mr. HASTERT. Yes, they did in many cases.

Mrs. COLLINS. Well——

Mr: HASTERT. It is my time. At the same time, that sport had rising growth rate in both elementary and secondary levels. Sixty-four men's swimming teams have disappeared. Water polo is down to 45 teams. It is not factual to say, in these cases, that men's sports have grown. They haven t. They have been the victims of Title IX.

Mr. GUNDERSON. Thank you.

Thank you, Mr. Chairman.

Chairman McKEON. Ms. Woolsey.

Ms. WOOLSEY. Thank you, Mr. Chairman,

I would like to approach this from a different angle. I am a mother of three sons and a daughter. One of my sons was a wrestler another was an All-State, both in high school and college, baseball player; the other, in college, Honorable Mention, all-American Tackle; and my daughter was a skater, a competitive skater. And I am absolutely certain that sports contributed a lot to molding all four of my children into very solid individuals as young adults.

I also know that is why they stayed out of trouble when they [were] in high school—they were busy, they were involved, they were doing something that was important to them, and they were too tired to get in trouble.

Also, before I came to Congress, I was a human resources professional, and it was very, very clear to me that the differences between young men and young women who graduated college and got into the business world, had a lot to do with whether or not they had learned teamwork, whether they had gained self-confidence and poise, and whether they had learned through something other than just reading books, how to get along in an atmosphere where you had to give and take, win and lose, and go forward.

The young people who had played sports had an advantage over those who didn't. Now, they could also be young people who played an instrument or did something other than just plain study out of a book.

My point here is, when we are talking about Title IX, not to take away something from the young men, but to bring women up to the same level. Women have to have the same advantages that men have when they enter the real world after college. And sports gives them scholarships, poise, and self-confidence. It is a learning experience, whether it involves team competition or individual competition, like my daughter, as a competitive skater.

I would just say that, if it is necessary to fix Title IX, we fix it by coming up to a higher level, not by going down to a lower level. We should do everything possible to give equal opportunities to both the young women and the young men.

Last year, I worked with you, Congresswoman Collins, on the athletic disclosure bill that was passed. I am wondering, now that the bill is law, has it had an impact and what have you seen from that?

Mrs. COLLINS. I believe that it has had an impact. One of the things that I have learned from speaking to people who are interested in the law, is they feel that it has enabled them to have sort of another prong from which to work to encourage young people who are really interested in getting into sports to know that they can, they have the opportunity to do so. I think it has worked, and I am very pleased with that.

Ms. WOOLSEY. I have a young woman in my district who is in high school who plays on the boys' football team. She and her mother came to me; they are very, very interested in what happens with this Title IX debate because she would like the opportunity to play football in college.

My son was an Honorable Mention, All-American Tackle. I would not want any other son to be tackled by him, much less a daughter.

Could you respond on women in contact sports?

Mr. HASTERT. That is up to the individual. It's the individual's choice. I know one of the people testifying today, T.J. Kerr, from California State at Bakersfield, has initiated a coed wrestling team and has had some success with it. I think that is an individual decision.

But you are right on point. I believe exactly what you believe, that we should expand the opportunities for women, not bring down the opportunities for men. In your State, in California, your sons today, with recent decisions in California, probably wouldn't have the same opportunities in wrestling and baseball that they would have had five or six years ago in college.

Ms. WOOLSEY. I know my time is up, but I would like to suggest that we bring this debate up to that level, that our goal be to equalize this, not to take something away from someone. As soon as we start pitting winners and losers against each other, we have lost the debate, because it won't work.

Mr. HASTERT. That is exactly my thesis, so I thank you.

Ms. WOOLSEY. Thank you, Mr. Hastert, and thank you, Mr. Chairman.

Chairman McKEON. I think that we may have been a little confrontational here, but I think that is because of the goal that we are working for. Just by bringing it up, I think we have rallied the troops and people are taking sides and fighting over a small piece of the pie, instead of saying what can be done to enhance the whole program.

As I gather from what Mr. Hastert was saying, first of all, not cutting one at the expense of another is how can we expand opportunities for all.

Mr. HASTERT. What has happened in reality is that the Department of Education, through the OCR, has given ultimatums to many schools saying, if you don't wish to expand a woman's sport, you drop two or three men's sports to get close to proportionality. We are saying that is not the intent of Title IX, it is wrong, and we should take another look at it.

Chairman McKEON. That is, I think, the whole purpose of this hearing. This hasn't been looked at for a number of years, and we are trying to determine what we can do to get everyone in the boat together. That is probably the biggest thing that I have been able to do in coming to Congress is say let's try to work together. This probably would be a good place to be doing it.

Mr. Roemer.

Mr. ROEMER. Thank you, Mr. Chairman.

I welcome my fellow colleague from the State of Illinois before our subcommittee this morning. Certainly many of us, if not all of us, on this subcommittee and in Congress, agree with the spirit of law of Title IX. We want to make sure that girls and women have the opportunities that boys and men have in our society.

As I go around the Third District of Indiana, I find more and more young girls are playing soccer, softball, baseball, yet many of these young women and girls have not yet moved into the college ranks to see this reciprocated and reflected at the collegiate level. For example, at the University of Notre Dame, we have 175 young men try out for the baseball team, and only 35 or 30 can make it. We have only 25 or 27 young women try out for the softball team, and most of them make it. We have one of the best women's softball teams in the country, ranked in the top 20, and we are very proud of that. How do we get this law to work so that we encourage more women at the University of Notre Dame, 175, to try out for the softball team and to make that softball team and maybe increase the numbers to 35 or 40, ultimately on the roster? How do other schools like the University of Iowa and the University of Washington accomplish much of Title IX without eliminating men's programs?

Mr. Hastert, you have said a couple of times that the OCR has required that men's programs be cut. How can you attribute this directly—and maybe you have information that I haven't seen yet—to Title IX rather than simply to some of the cost-cutting that is currently going on at many universities?

Mr. HASTERT. Because in specific instances, when the administration decides to cut a sport because of cost-cutting, just drop a sport and say it is because of cost-cutting. Others have been taken to court and entered in with OCR and had a consent decree or some type of an agreement that OCR will back off their court case if they drop two men's sports.

Mr. ROEMER. And you have seen this in writing from OCR?

Mr. HASTERT. President Jorns from Eastern Illinois University will testify today that that happened in his school, and through our efforts they reengaged the OCR so that they did make a change. I believe Northern Illinois University said that if they expanded one women's sport and dropped two men's sports, then the OCR would back off their case. It is there. It happens time after time, after time, after time.

Mr. ROEMER. I would certainly like to see the proof of that in writing—not that I question what you have said at all—but I will ask the same question to the representatives of the Department of Education's OCR office, and I appreciate your answer.

Representative Collins, let me ask you a question. You certainly have made a very compelling case that we have not complied, that we have a long way to go. What suggestions would you have for us to improve opportunities for women at the collegiate level, and, as I gave the example earlier, how do we encourage young girls to get involved so that we don't see this problem later on?

Mrs. COLLINS. I would like to see OCR begin to take some of these cases to court themselves, rather than having the young girls do so. Then I would like to see the Federal Government deny some of these universities Federal funds. I believe if that were to happen, they would all begin to look at the law and say, well, we are going to be in compliance. Until that happens, I think you are still going to have these arguments, I think you are still going to have people ignoring Title IX, and I think you are still going to have the same problems, where you have the school administrators, you have the NCAA, which, of course, as you know, is composed of the school administrators and the athletic directors and coaches, doing the same things that they are doing now. There has to be something to give them a jolt to let them know that we are very serious about giving young women an opportunity.

It was said here that perhaps we ought to raise funding or create some kind of a mechanism by which the men can stay where they are. But we know the Federal funds aren't there. Who are we fooling? We are kidding ourselves if we think the money is going to drop out of the sky. The money isn't going to drop out of the sky. I think we need to give enforcement a big try. That is what I would like to see happen.

Mr. HASTERT. But you will note that there are a lot of programs, such as at Notre Dame and at others across the country, that offer women slots, scholarship slots, but don't have enough women interested in participating. The interest isn't there, so in order to meet proportionality, they start to cap the number of walk-ons and cap men's participation, which doesn't cost the school any money at all—

Mrs. COLLINS. But there are schools where there is a great deal of interest. Why do you think we have had these court cases? The women have gone to court saying they want to play soccer saying they want to have a swimming team, saying they want to play squash or have archery. They want to have these various kinds of sports, and they have been denied the opportunity.

You can always point to one or two isolated incidents and say they are indicative of what is happening across university campuses all over the world. Not the case. I believe we have to have enforcement. I believe the OCR is the place to do it, and until that happens, you are going to have these kinds of problems.

Mr. ROEMER. Thank you, Mr. Chairman

Chairman MCKEON. Thank you.

Mr. Barrett would like to acknowledge a member of his State before he has to leave for another meeting.

Mr. BARRETT. I thank the Chairman for recognizing me.

As a Member of the full Committee on Economic and Educational Opportunities, it is a pleasure to be able to sit in for a moment in this hearing today which is important to so many people. I want to take a minute to reflect on the subcommittee's records that Dr. Tom Osborne, the Coach of the National Champion Nebraska Corn Huskers is in the audience today. As many of you know he is the winningest active college football coach in the Nation and was just voted the National Coach of the Year. I think it is significant that he is here today because of the continuing interest in a program that has been successful.

And perhaps following up on Mr. Hastert's comments—while we need to encourage, and should encourage, access to viable athletic programs, we also need to be careful because we are walking a very fine line not to penalize successful programs.

So, I want to thank the Chairman for allowing me to introduce a friend of mine who the last time we met was at the White House when Dr. Osborne had his winning Nebraska Corn Huskers in Washington to meet the President a couple of months ago. I wonder if Dr. Osborne would please stand and be recognized.

Mr. BARRETT. Thank you, Mr. Chairman.

Chairman McKEON. Thank you.

Mr. Reed.

Mr. REED. I have no questions.

Chairman McKEON. I think that concludes all the questions——

Mrs. MINK. Could I ask a question of our colleague Mr. Hastert?

Mr. WILLIAMS. Mr. Chairman, I ask unanimous consent that the gentlelady, not a Member of this subcommittee, be recognized for one question.

Mrs. MINK. I know that the Office of Civil Rights will be testifying also and presenting their side. I am very much interested in your statement that with respect to Eastern Illinois, that the university was given only one avenue to satisfy Title IX, and that was the question of proportionality.

The summaries that I have here indicate that there were no increases in women's athletic opportunities at the university since 1978, and that, taking that note, which was one of the three in the regulations that you need to comply with, OCR searched for areas which might very well meet the other requirements in the regulations. And in searching for aspects of qualifications with respect to the other two, OCR found that women students had requested establishment of programs and were ignored by the university. So, in contrast to the illustration that at Notre Dame, programs were set up, but women were not interested in participating, at Eastern Illinois, specific requests by women athletes were ignored, and no new programs were established for women since 1978.

Could you comment on that?

Mr. HASTERT. First of all, President Jorns will testify on behalf of Eastern Illinois. He is certainly an expert on that situation. My understanding was that one of the sports that was demanded to be put in place was field hockey. That is not an indigenous sport to Illinois; it is more of an East Coast sport.

In addition, the OCR said, you eliminate two men's sports. It is the elimination of men's sports that I think is egregious here. And I think it is fine to grow women's sports as much as possible. I have always been an advocate of that. But to meet proportionality by eliminating men's sports is wrong, whether it happens in Illinois, or in Ohio, or in Hawaii, or in California. It is wrong to do that.

Mrs. MINK. Thank you, Mr. Chairman.

Chairman MCKEON. Mr. Ewing.

Mr. EWING. Thank you, Mr. Chairman. I appreciate being able to participate as an observer and to have a question in your subcommittee. I thought maybe I ought to be sitting out there between my two colleagues from Illinois, both my good friends.

Congresswoman Collins, you seem to indicate that you would advocate more court cases to try to bring this into equality, the equality that you think is lacking. Recently, a university in my district dropped a male sport and added the same sport on the women's side. Would it not be then that the male athletes who can no longer play soccer should be going to court to try to show that they have been denied rights because we now have women's soccer.

Mrs. COLLINS. The court system is open to everybody. That is the way of our country.

Mr. EWING. I realize that, but do you think that will get to the goal of equality? In this case, whatever the reason, whether financial or to come into compliance, they had decided that they will add women's sports and cut men's sports to try to meet the guidelines of the law and their budget requirements. But who does it leave out? It leaves out male athletes who were involved in that sport.

Mrs. COLLINS. Who was left out before? It was the women who wanted to play soccer.

Mr. EWING. Is that equality, though, to change where the discrimination lies?

Mrs. COLLINS. It is not equality, but it equalizes the men and women who want to play. You have both playing. However, if a young man wants to go to court, he is welcome to go to court. That is what our system is for. Perhaps they will rule in his favor. He ought to take it to court if he wants to.

Mr. EWING. That leaves the university with coming back to cut a women's sport then?

Mrs. COLLINS. They should have done the right thing in the first place. It gets them off the hook by saying we have taken this case to court and the judge is going to decide, rather than the administrator of the university making a decision before that time.

Mr. EWING. One follow-up question, Congresswoman. Would you think that there could be a better way to determine the interest between the sexes for sports than just saying you have 50 percent women or 52 percent women, you will have

52 percent slots for females and 48 for men? Do you think there is a better way that we can truly avoid—the point you made very aptly—both sides going to court? Our courts are clogged with a lot of other things.

Mrs. Collins. I am interested in hearing suggestions that may be out there. I have given my suggestions for more than four years on this case. I would like to hear what others have to say. I want to hear them say that football is not sacrosanct and that there is an opportunity for women to participate in sports on an equal basis with men.

Mr. Ewing. Thank you.

Thank you, Mr. Chairman.

Chairman McKeon. Thank you.

Football is not sacrosanct.

Mrs. Collins. Is that asking too much, Mr. Chairman?

Chairman McKeon. I wish we weren't on national television. I would like to talk about this a little bit. In some places it is.

You said you were interested in ideas. One of the comments that was made earlier is that the reasons why we have athletics are that benefits are derived from teamwork and that participation and exercise builds up your muscles. A lot of benefits come from athletics.

You know, I went to Brigham Young University, and one of the things that they did when I went to school was to offer a very good intermural sports program that really enlarged the opportunities. I had great interest, just was never a very good player. But through the intermural sports that they had broadly throughout the school, we were able to participate and get all the other benefits, even though we were never, some of us, able to play on a par that would enable us to play on one of the major teams. That is one possible suggestion where you could get all of the benefits that came from sports, except for the very top competitors—most of them, it seems—at university levels go on to professional sports at some level. We appreciate—

Mr. Hastert. Could I say one thing and follow up on what Congressman Ewing said, and the encouragement by Representative Collins to go to court? A lot of colleges and universities have a limited amount of money to spend on education—and that pie gets smaller all the time—and are intimidated by being pushed into court. Just as we saw in other types of liability and tort reform cases, the very threat of going to court and having to spend $1 million, or $1.5 or $2 million that they need to spend for the education of young people, to defend themselves in court, in a Federal court against a Federal Agency, they don't see that they can win.

The way the law has been construed and the precedents set by the Federal court, this is an intimidator. So I understand why my good friend from Illinois wants to push people who feel they weren't given a fair shake into Federal courts—because precedents have been set, and the schools would rather settle than spend very precious dollars that could be spent on education trying to defend themselves in Federal court.

Mrs. Collins. Mr. Chairman, I would hate to think that the Federal court is an intimidator. That is strong language. It seems to me that Federal courts are out there to be fair to all people. That is pretty heavy.

Chairman MCKEON. Pretty heavy, and I think probably has a great deal of truth.

Mrs. COLLINS. Yes, but let me tell you something; I would hate to think that.

Chairman MCKEON. I want to thank you for bringing this up.

Congressman Hastert, it was your attention that brought this debate and brought this hearing, and I appreciate your doing that. We will excuse the present panel now and move to the next panel.

Thank you very much.

PREPARED TESTIMONY OF T. J. KERR ON BEHALF OF THE NATIONAL WRESTLING COACHES ASSOCIATION PRESENTED TO THE POSTSECONDARY EDUCATION SUBCOMMITTEE UNITED STATES HOUSE OF REPRESENTATIVES

May 9, 1995

The Coalition's Position Regarding the Office for Civil Rights' Interpretation and Enforcement of Title IX

Summary

1. we support Title IX and the Congressional intent to prohibit discrimination based on gender.

2. We oppose and object to the OCR's interpretation and manner of enforcing Title IX, particularly that portion which stresses the proportionality rule. The proportionality rule is a gender quota which ties athletic participation ratios to enrollment ratios.

3. As a direct consequence of OCR interpretation and enforcement policies, school administrators feel compelled to drop male sports programs rather than add female sports programs.

4. For example, the number of male gymnastics programs has now slipped to fewer than 40, the minimum number required to hold an NCAA tournament. When a sport loses its NCAA tournament extinction at the college level is inevitable. The imminent extinction of male gymnastics has to be the result of the gender quota in that *female* gymnastics at the college level is thriving.

5. All male sports programs are vulnerable in that approximately half of the nearly 200,000 of the male college athletes must be eliminated to reach the gender quota.

6. The OCR maintains that it places no more emphasis on the proportionality rule (prong 1) than the other two prongs. The other prongs, *as interpreted and*

enforced by the OCR, however, are but facades to avoid the prohibition against quotas announced in the *Bakke* decision.

7. The unfair and discriminatory OCR rules are creating anger and resentment among males and those rules will soon have an extraordinarily deleterious effect on our Olympic efforts and the character of our high school, junior high and grade school boys.

Introduction

Mr. Chairman and members of the Subcommittee I am T.J. Kerr, wrestling coach at California State University at Bakersfield and President of the National Wrestling Coaches Association (NWCA). I am honored and privileged that you selected me to address you today about a crisis within our athletic community.

The NWCA is the voice of all wrestling coaches in the country. I shall also attempt to speak on behalf of all the young male athletes in this nation and their parents. We are particularly concerned about the tens of thousands of young men whose athletic careers have already been cut short by the OCR rules.

While we firmly agree with the letter and the spirit of Title IX, we are firmly committed to the proposition that it is unconscionable to eliminate male programs or male athletes to satisfy a gender quota. Both the OCR and the courts have expressed the opinion that a school is justified in dropping male athletes in order to comply with Title IX. We believe that this opinion misconstrues Congressional intent.

We are today therefore petitioning Congress seeking relief from the draconian but unintended consequences of Title IX as interpreted and enforced by the OCR and the courts.

Is There A Crisis?

As a threshold issue, you might ask—is there a crisis? Yes there is. Male gymnastics is almost extinct at the college level. Wrestling has relatively recently lost over 100 programs and may lose as many as 20 programs this year.

Programs in every sport have been dropped or reduced in number—soccer, baseball, tennis, swimming. etc.—even football and basketball.

Why Is There A Crisis?

All male sports programs are at risk because of the proportionality rule/gender quota which the OCR has drafted. There are about 190,000 male college athletes in Divisions I, II, and III. There are about 105,000 female athletes. How can proportionality be achieved when the present male to female ratio is 47–53? If the trend continues, administrators will have to eliminate about 100,000 male athletes to reach proportionality.

In 1972 when Congress enacted Title IX the college enrollment ratio nationally was 55%+ male. By the 21st Century 55% of the college population may well be female. The 55–45 female-to-male ratio sets up a gender quota which is impossible to achieve in no small part because females do not tend to compete in sports—particularly those like football and wrestling. Nor do they participate in a non-scholarship/walk-on capacity in anywhere near the number which males do. California Bakersfield, for example, we are 62% female by enrollment. Statistically, it is almost impossible with that enrollment ratio to have a viably diverse athletics program for male students.

How Does Proportionality Cause Elimination?

Elimination of male athletes occurs in two ways—administrators eliminate *programs* and/or they eliminate *non-scholarship/walk-ons athletes* from those programs. Both are anathema. We have one goal—We seek to end the elimination or reduction of male sports programs to achieve a quota.

School administrators believe that they must achieve proportionality. Many are unable, because of budget constraints, to add female sports programs, so these administrators drop male programs or "cap" sports by dropping the non-scholarship or walk-on athlete.

Both of these approaches to achieving "gender equity" are wrong. Programs should not be eliminated because athletes matriculate at a school in the good faith belief that the administration will honor its commitment to provide a program for their four years of college. It is a devastating betrayal for these young men when they learn that their faith has been misplaced. It is worse when they are informed that the reason for the elimination of their program is Title IX or gender equity.

The capping of male sports is equally discriminatory and destructive. In this circumstance a young man pays tuition, walks on to a team, works as hard as the first-teamer, but simply does not have the skills to compete at the highest levels. These athletes normally are the best students and the best contributors to their alma maters when they graduate. More importantly, they are comparatively free to the school. The school dumps them because they are the most expendable.

Why Is The Proportionality Rule The Only (Real) Rule?

The OCR's Director, Norma Cantu, has claimed on many occasions that administrators need not eliminate male programs to satisfy Title IX. She says that administrators can satisfy any of the prongs to comply with Title IX. All administrators—even her supporters—disagree (see below).

Initially, almost everyone "knows" that prongs 2 and 3 simply avoid the sanctions of the Bakke decision which prohibits gender quotas. As interpreted and applied by the OCR the prongs are nothing but a facade. Prong 2 dictates that administrators gravitate toward the gender quota, a standard that most can not meet by adding women's sports programs.

Prong 3 is the interest and abilities prong. By any measure of interest thus far tested, males show a far greater interest in sports participation than females at all levels, The OCR, however, ignores these measures. Probably no school has ever met this test to OCR's satisfaction.

Ironically, even Norma Cantu's supporters unwittingly contradict her about the primacy of the proportionality rule. In a letter to Senator Breaux dated January 25, 1995 the 600+ members of the National Association of Collegiate Women Athletic Administrators (NACWAA) wrote:

> "HOW CAN IT BE? that certain members of the United States Senate who profess to support gender equity could suggest that Secretary Riley reject the proportionality test as a <u>primary measure of compliance with Title IX. [W]hen judges in more than ten major Title IX court cases to date have determined that proportionality is the single most important prong of the three pronged test of compliance.</u>"

At the very least, NACWAA's letter contradicts Ms. Cantu's position and corroborates our position—the proportionality rule is dispositive of compliance with Title IX, and that is what all administrators think too.

What Is The Impact Of The Gender Quota On Our Next Generation Of Male Athletes?

I have sought in my program to work with many young men who otherwise would not be able to attend college, and I know I speak for the coaches of all male programs when I say that the elimination of male opportunities will greatly affect the future generation of young men.

All statistics reflect that the opportunities existing for females is much greater than for males. For example, wrestling is the sixth most popular high school sport in the nation. There is, however only one college program for every 33 high school wrestling programs (33–1). Of the top ten female sports, the worst ratio is about 22–1 and the best ratio is about 11–1. High school females have greater opportunities to compete at every collegiate level in every counterpart sport except golf and gymnastics.

As these disparities continue to grow as male programs are eliminated, high school and junior high school male programs will atrophy and die. Many kids, without the option of participating in athletics, will choose antisocial activities.

Unfortunately, at present there is hardly a male high school athlete who is unaware of Title IX and the OCR's approach to gender equality. Expectedly these males are angry and their morale is sinking.

What Is The Impact Of The Gender Quota On Our Olympic Teams?

The vast majority of our Olympic athletes have trained in the university. If, for example, gymnastics is allowed to die at the college level, the quality of our Olympic team will be greatly reduced. Does this Congress want this to be another unintended consequence of Title IX interpretation and enforcement?

What Other Problems Has The OCR's Gender Quota Created?

Ironically, as a direct consequence of the OCR's and NOW's pressure the California State University system signed a consent decree requiring proportionality by 1998. At Cal State Bakersfield male Olympic sports are all but doomed. Recently, San Francisco State dropped its football team. NOW has signed a similar contract with the Chicago school system and Florida has created a statute revolving around the proportionality rule.

Another irony is that while my wrestling program creates a great deal of its own revenue, we are required to give 50% of what we earn to the female programs, obviously donors want to give their money to a particular program and when they learn that half of their money is going to another program (whether male or female) they refuse to donate anything. Furthermore, our athletes have come to resent the fact that we have to work both for our own program and help to fund the programs which do not work to fund themselves.

What Is OCR's Definition Of "Participant"—And Why Is That Definition Destroying Male Sports Opportunities?

A very important issue in the analysis of OCR's gender quota is how the term "participant" is to be defined. Presently the OCR defines participant as either a scholarship or non-scholarship athlete.

Since male sports programs encourage walk-ons to try out for the teams, there are probably more non-scholarship male athletes than scholarship athletes.

On the other hand, there are far fewer females who participate in a non-scholarship capacity. At the Division III level, for example—where all athletes are non-scholarship—male athletes outnumber female athletes by 25,000 participants.

The irony is that in the OCR's "final solution" it is permissible to achieve "gender equity" by simply eliminating these male non-scholarship athletes. It is true that by eliminating all male walk-ons we could achieve proportionality. But we could also achieve proportionality by requiring females to fill their "unused participatory opportunities." Which is the better solution? To eliminate or create participatory slots?

The obvious reason why non-scholarship female athletic slots are not presently created is that coaches of female programs know that they do not have to encourage walk-ons or even permit them to try out in that their schools *must* provide additional slots. The females therefore have the leverage to require the schools to create only scholarship participatory slots.

Again, administrators, in order to retain discretionary control over their schools simply eliminate male athletes by capping sports.

What Can Be Done To Solve The Problem?

First, things have changed since 1972 when Title IX was enacted. Female athletic participation has skyrocketed from about 10% to about 40% of the total collegiate athletic community. These enormous changes occurred in the face of the fact that football, a non-counterpart sport, absorbs over 1/4 of all of the male participation slots.

"Gender equity" is a reality in almost every school in the country. As proof, one need only reflect on the fact that females now have nearly the same number of college athletic programs as males (6520–7211 respectively) and receive more scholarship aid in almost every counterpart sport.

Gender equity, however, should not be synonymous with gender quotas. The OCR's gender quota, which masquerades as the proportionality rule, is now an anachronism which should be abolished.

In its place, reason should prevail. Schools offering the same number of athletic programs to males and females should be deemed to be in compliance with Title IX. Since there are nearly the same number of athletic programs presently for males and females, schools should be encouraged to build up the present programs rather than creating new ones.

Also, in that males participate in a non-scholarship/walk-on capacity in much greater numbers than females, it is time to require females to fill these "unused participatory opportunities" which if developed, would solve this problem alone.

Conclusion

In conclusion, Mr. Chairman, thank you for holding this hearing to consider our petition. I know that when you created Title IX you did not intend the elimination of male sports as we know them—that, however, will be the unintended consequence if Congress does not intervene. We need your help to change the rules so that we can exist and make gender equity work for both males and females.

Finally, thank you for the opportunity to appear here today. I will be happy to answer to the best of my ability any questions you may have of me.

THE OCR IS DESTROYING MALE SPORT OPPORTUNITIES

The Problem

Title IX, enacted in 1972, prohibits gender discrimination in educational settings.

In 1979 the Education Department's Office for Civil Rights (OCR) created a three-part test to measure compliance with Title IX. The Director of the OCR, Norma Cantu, has on several occasions, stated that a school can comply with any of the prongs to be in compliance with Title IX. The problem is that, as interpreted and enforced by the OCR, prongs 2 and 3 are merely facades to avoid the prohibition against gender quotas which the Supreme Court announced in the *Bakke* decision. The prongs are:

1. Are the participation opportunities for women and men substantially proportionate to their respective rates of enrollment?

    Presently, female enrollment nationally is 53%. Female athletic participation nationally is about 37% (105,000). To create proportionality educational administrators must raise female participation to 53% (200,000), lower male participation to 47% (from the current 190,000 to 100,000) or create some combination therof.

    Impact on Male Sports

    This "proportionality rule" is a quota that can not be met without destroying male sports programs primarily because females do not tend to:

    > compete in certain sports—like football and . . . wrestling—which have historically attracted large numbers of student-athletes

    > compete at the college level in a non-scholarship or "walk-on" capacity

    The facts that football teams are large and that females do not tend to compete in a non-scholarship capacity in anywhere near the numbers of males tend to skew the participation ratios greatly towards men and make compliance with the proportionality rule nearly impossible.

2. Has there been a continuing practice of program expansion for the under-represented sex?

    Since almost no school with a football team can satisfy the gender quota required by the OCR under part 1 all schools must satisfy part 2. The OCR and the courts require that schools show the addition of "recent" new female programs. Also, since it is nearly impossible to add enough female programs to reach proportionality (primarily because of the football numbers and the females tendency to not walk-on), this approach puts educational administrators on the OCR treadmill virtually forever.

Impact on Male Sports

Educational administrators—realizing that the gender quota can never be reached (under part #1) by adding female athletic teams—have decided to just drop their male teams and/or athletes. Dropping male athletes has the additional benefits of avoiding endless regulation by the OCR which occurs when a school takes the program expansion approach. (Also, elimination of programs puts extra money in to the administrative budgets.)

3. Has the school fully and effectively accommodated the interests and abilities of the under-represented sex?

When schools are out of proportion they normally can not meet this prong no matter how many surveys they do or how powerfully they show that the disparity is not based on discrimination. Probably no school has ever passed this test to the satisfaction of the OCR. Conversely, if a female team steps forward and demands NCAA status, the school realistically must instate the team. The reason is that since the school is out of proportion the administrators must get in proportion. The females are obviously interested and there is no way to test ability.

Impact on Male Sports

This standard is the most unfair and the most likely to result in administrators' eliminating male sports. This standard never benefits males or administrators.

For example, now that bowling is an NCAA sport, a group of female bowlers can demand that their college administrators instate them as a team and give them all of the resources of any other NCAA athletic team. Administrators are vulnerable and must acquiesce regardless of the bowling averages of the female students because there is no standard to test abilities.

Other classic examples are the sports of female crew and lacrosse which usually have no high school base in the states where the universities instate the teams.

In order to avoid even the possibility that a few female student-athletes can dictate university policy, most administrators will inevitably decide to simply drop male sports programs.

The Elimination of Male Athletic Opportunities

Males are being deprived of an opportunity to participate in college sports and being discriminated against because of the gender quota set by the Office for Civil Rights in two separate and distinct ways:

1. male athletic *programs* are being eliminated; and

2. *"walk-ons"/non-scholarship athletes* are being eliminated.

The Elimination of Male Athletic Programs

Numerous male sports programs have been dropped recently as a result of the gender quota created by the Office for Civil Rights.

The most dramatic example of this phenomenon is male gymnastics. Within the 40 teams, the least number required to maintain an NCAA tournament. Meanwhile, female gymnastics at the college level flourishes. Almost all of male Olympic gymnasts are selected from the college ranks so this attrition will inevitably affect our Olympic efforts.

All of the other male sports programs are also inexorably being drawn toward this black hole of extinction created by the OCR. Wrestling, for instance, has lost about 140 programs.

Nationally, there are about 190,000 male college athletes and about 105,000 female athletes. Since female students outnumber male students nationally (53%–47%), OCR's gender quota requires that there be more female athletes than male athletes. So educational administrators must either add 100,000 female athletes, eliminate 100,000 male athletes or some combination thereof. If administrators continue to choose "elimination"—even in combination with adding female sports programs—all male Olympic athletic programs will be destroyed before the gender quota can be satisfied.

The Elimination of Male "Walk-ons"—Capping Sports Programs

A more insidious approach to eliminating sports opportunities for males is to "cap" sports programs. This term means that walk-ons/non-scholarship athletes are dumped for the sole purpose of moving toward a gender quota. Non-scholarship/walk-on athletes cost the university virtually nothing, generally maintain the highest grade point average among athletes and are the most generous contributors upon graduation.

The real problem here is the manner in which OCR defines and counts "participants." All athletes, whether scholarship or not, are "bean-counted" the same. The real effect is that coaches of female programs coaches know that universities must increase female participation. These coaches must be given the option and must decide whether to increase their teams with scholarship or non-scholarship athletes. The obvious result is that female programs usually refuse to encourage, and in many cases will not take on, walk-ons. Schools are then required to fill all female teams with scholarship athletes—or eliminate male non-scholarship athletes.

Presently there are tens of thousands more male than female non-scholarship/walk-on athletes. Since females now have almost as many teams as males do nationally (6520 female programs to 7211 male programs), they should be required to fill their "unused participatory slots" before seeking more scholarship slots.

Conclusion—Solution

Somewhere along the way the OCR's interpretation and enforcement of Title IX has lost a basic sense of reality and common sense. The purpose of Title IX is to fight discrimination. How does the elimination of male sports programs and athletes help to end discrimination?

Young male athletes arrive on campus every fall in the good-faith belief that they have an agreement with the university that they will be able to compete in their sports and their parents hope they will mature into men. The trauma visited upon these athletes when they are informed that they (or their sports programs) have been dropped is impossible to explain. The administrators' rationale that it is the government's gender quota which has destroyed their opportunity to participate creates extraordinary disillusionment, anger and frustration. Is it any wonder why our kids and our citizenry distrust and dislike our government bureaucracies?

We are petitioning Congress because Congress created a well-intentioned statute which worked reasonably well in the 80's to help increase female athletic opportunities. However, the unintended consequences of the 90's is that the OCR's rules, regulations and enforcement policies will destroy male athletics, do little to help females and will inevitably create extraordinary polarization primarily between the genders.

The problem, in greatest part, has been precipitated by the fact that the OCR, headed by Norma Cantu, has been, is, and will always be apparently unconcerned by the fate of male athletics.

It is therefore crucial that Congress clarify its intent regarding discrimination— that is: *Title IX was created to prohibit discrimination against females—not to destroy opportunities for males.*

Specifically, we ask that Congress consider the following proposals:

Proposals

1. abolish OCR's gender quota. There is no logical reason for the continuing existence of the proportionality rule. Most importantly, there is no relationship between enrollment gender ratios and athletic participation ratios. Initially, the quota had the beneficent effect of quickly raising female participation rates to nearly 40%. It has now reached a point of greatly diminishing returns.

   "Gender equity" is now an integral part of almost every school in the country. The necessity to perpetuate a quota which is creating reverse discrimination, extraordinary discord and resentment has long since passed.

Until OCR's gender quota is abolished—

a. Colleges should be deemed in compliance with Title IX by offering the same number of programs to females as males. Again, schools now nationally offer nearly as many athletic programs nationally to females (6520) as males (7211).

b. Football (and other) teams which *do* create the revenue for the other sports to exist should be exempted. It is unfair to the other male sports programs to count football as part of the gender quota but not count the fact that *if* football is financially successful it is going to use more participatory slots and spend more money.

c. "Participants" should be defined as scholarship athletes only. Alternatively, females should be required to fill their "unused participatory slots" before creating new teams.

2. The proportionality test should be one of many criteria to assess whether new female athletic programs should be established.

PREPARED STATEMENT OF CHARLES M. NEINAS EXECUTIVE DIRECTOR COLLEGE FOOTBALL ASSOCIATION

My name is Charles Neinas and I am the executive director of the College Football Association. The CFA is comprised of 67 universities that are classified in NCAA Division 1-A which designates the most competitive classification in the sport of football. The CFA was founded in 1977 to provide a forum for universities to address subjects that are of particular interest to those involved in what is termed major college football. The CFA encourages the chief executive officers, faculty representatives, athletics directors and football coaches to work together on a common agenda. Through the years, the CFA has been in the forefront in strengthening academic standards, establishing restrictive rules governing recruiting and in the promotion of college football.

The Board of Directors of the CFA (roster attached) is most appreciative of the committee's willingness to consider what impact Title IX and the activities of the Office for Civil Rights (OCR) have upon college athletics. While created to consider matters related to major college football, our interest extends to college football at all levels as well as intercollegiate athletics for both men and women.

My primary mission today is to encourage continued congressional review of Title IX and to analyze the appropriateness of the interpretations and regulations that were adopted 20 years ago. In view of the changing landscape of intercollegiate athletics and the continuing progress that has been made in the development and growth of women's sports, there should be consideration as to whether the guidelines and Policy Interpretations of OCR reflect the current state of intercollegiate athletics.

For the record, let me state the following:

1. We DO NOT seek repeal of Title IX.

2. We DO NOT seek changes that would hinder the development of women's athletics.

3. We DO NOT seek exemption of football from Title IX.

4. We DO seek practical and reasonable interpretations and guidelines from OCR to eliminate colleges and universities from becoming prisoners to a strict proportionality test.

OCR established three tests in determining compliance with Title IX: proportionality, history of development and interest and abilities. Although OCR repeats that it utilizes the three tests in determining compliance, it is apparent by its actions that OCR considers the history of development and the interests and abilities tests as intermediate measures in reaching proportionality.

We believe that the unique size of college football teams needs to be taken into consideration as the Office for Civil Rights Policy Interpretations of 1979 promised.

> At several institutions, intercollegiate football is *unique* among sports. The *size* of the teams, the expense of the operation, and the revenue produced distinguish football from other sports, both men's and women's. Title IX requires that "an institution must comply with the prohibition against sex discrimination imposed by that title and its implementing regulations in the administration of any revenue producing intercollegiate athletic activity." However, the unique size and cost of football programs have been taken into account in developing this Policy Interpretations (Policy Interpretations, Section IX, Appendix A, paragraph 5, 71419).

Clearly, football was intended to be covered by Title IX, and the cost of certain aspects is what the Javits Amendment required as sex neutral considerations; i.e., the fact that football would cost more is not discriminatory. However, the unique size of college football teams is not taken into consideration by the Policy Interpretations, and the result is that current interpretations by OCR and the courts in imposing strict proportionality is narrow and unworkable.

At the time the Policy Interpretations was developed (by a panel of "experts" comprised of university presidents, athletics directors, representatives of women's athletic organizations, OCR attorneys and others), women's sports were governed by the Association of Intercollegiate Athletics for Women (AIAW) and men's sports were governed by the National Collegiate Athletic Association (NCAA) and the National Association of Intercollegiate Athletics (NAIA). These organizations had conflicting rules and interests. It is our belief that one of the reasons the section on the "effective accommodation of interests and abilities" has been the subject of controversy and conflicting interpretation is the diverse interest represented by those involved in drafting the Policy Interpretations in the late 1970s.

The first part of the three-part test, proportionality, originated as a threshold assumption of compliance. It was never intended to be an ultimate goal. The first OCR Investigator's Manual of 1980 made that clear, "Title IX does not require institutions to offer . . . a proportional number of intercollegiate participation opportunities" (1980 Investigators Manual, page 122, second paragraph). The proportionality test was adopted from OCR's experiences in the desegregation of school districts where it adopted a substantial proportionality test, not the strict proportionality test utilized in connection with Title IX.

If a strict proportionality measurement is used, what is the relevant pool to be surveyed, the entire student population or those that have a demonstrated interest in athletics? There have been a number of surveys undertaken by reputable sources in an attempt to distinguish if there is a difference in the interest in athletic participation between men and women. Studies by the U.S. Department of Education, The Educational Testing Service and Cooperative Institutional Research Programs at UCLA, as well as participation statistics by the National Federation of State High School Associations consistently reveal *a higher athletic interest among males* than females.

The five percent or less standard considered in Title IX cases appears to have originated from an out-of-court settlement of various lawsuits (e.g., *Sanders vs. University of Texas*) that is neither practical nor workable in institutions that sponsor football or have a larger percentage of females in the undergraduate enrollment.

The second test (i.e., history of development) is rarely taken into account by OCR or the courts. This test calls for the following:

> ". . . whether the institution can show a continuing practice of program expansion which is demonstrably responsive to the developing interests and abilities of members of that sex."

As is evident throughout an analysis of the Policy Interpretations, OCR has not developed any policy clarification to define what constitutes a history of continuing practice of program expansion.

When Title IX was implemented, many colleges and universities accelerated the development of women's programs and initiated several sports. For example, Brown University, which currently sponsors 17 sports for women, actually started 13 sports for women within a short period of time in the 1970s. Brown and other institutions that made an early commitment to women's athletics have received no credit for what they have accomplished in the development of women's sports on campus. In fact, such institutions are penalized for their history of promoting women's sports. It would seem entirely appropriate that the second test focus on history AND development rather than utilizing only program expansion.

The third test (i.e. interests and abilities) may appear to provide institutions that sponsor football the opportunity to be in compliance, but not in the manner in which it is currently being interpreted by OCR. The test provides:

> ". . . whether it can be demonstrated that the interests and abilities of the members of that sex have been fully and effectively accommodated by the present program."

It would appear logical and reasonable to assess the voluntary activities on the campus through a review of participation in club sports or intramural activities. Also, consideration should be given to those sports that are popular at the high school level in the area in which the institution is located. Utilizing such analysis, an institution could determine if there was unmet interest, but OCR continues to emphasize strict proportionality by making the third test more difficult to satisfy. Institutions are now being required to consider the athletic interests of *potential* students (those that may or may not attend the university) in accommodating the interests of actual students at the university. The rationale of such an approach is difficult to understand. For example, if a particular women's sport is played in one part of the country but is not popular in another part of the country, what is the institution's obligation? The Eastern Illinois case is an example where OCR declared that the university must add field hockey for women although the sport is not played in the area in which the institution is located. It is absurd to add varsity sports absent any demonstrated interest and ability within a particular institution.

The 1980 Investigator's Manual states: "The absence of expressed interests by women . . . may often be a sign that the institution needs to increase the awareness of women of athletic opportunities and to develop club, intramural and recreational programs for women" (1980 Investigator's Manual, page 128). We support this approach. Creation of opportunities in such a manner could allow women's sports to blossom or fade, and that is the true test of interest.

At one time the number of sports offered men at a university far exceeded the sports offerings for women. This is no longer true! At many institutions the number of sports for women are equal to or greater than the number of sports offered for men.

Also, it is not true that the overall growth of women's programs has not been at the expense of men's sports. Universities have had to accommodate the need to expand programs and increase opportunities for women and in so doing eliminated men's sports for a variety of reasons. For example, during the past ten years, 64 NCAA members have discontinued men's swimming. Over the last 20 years, the number of wrestling programs in the NCAA has been reduced from 401 to 261. A survey of CFA members indicates that in the last ten years there have been 123 sports added for women and 39 sports for men have been discontinued.

Perhaps the greatest fallacy of all lies in the assertion that the unique size of college football programs was taken into account in the development of the Policy Interpretations. As discussed earlier, this simply is not true. Another problem with the Policy Interpretations is that it makes no distinction between the different division levels. While the I-A and I-AA distinctions are for the sport of football, most institutions competing at each level have different funding sources. Many of the Division I-A institutions have fully funded women's programs that benefit tremendously from the existence of football and the revenue that is generated through gate receipts, television and donors to the athletic program whose primary interest is college football. Those universities where football teams compete at the I-AA level do not have the same funding resources but also do not have as many scholarships or coaches. These institutions depend heavily on financial contributions from alumni and fund raising to support their intercollegiate teams because they do not enjoy the same level of attendance or interest.

The problem of strict proportionality impacts upon all institutions sponsoring the sport of football whether it be at the Division IA level or Division III. Footballs, helmets and shoulder pads cost the same whether you are buying equipment for the University of Nebraska or Central College of Pella, Iowa. The Nebraskas, Penn States and Notre Dames of the world will continue to sponsor football because it is the primary source of income that funds the entire athletic program and also serves as a public relations and fund raising instrument for the university as a whole. Other men's sports at such institutions, however, may suffer as a result. It is when you talk about those programs sponsored at the Division II and the Division III level of the NCAA that football is in jeopardy of being discontinued.

There are two indisputable facts when comparing participation rates between men's and women's sports. First, football requires and attracts a larger number of participants. The overall average squad size in the sport of football ranges from 117 at the Division I-A level to 77 at the Division III level. Second, more men are interested in participating in intercollegiate athletics than women, even though at the Division I level there is more financial aid available per capita and absolute dollars for the women in matched sports. An analysis of the 1993–1994 participation study by the NCAA illustrates the point. Comparing like sports at the Division I level (basketball, cross country, fencing, golf, gymnastics, lacrosse, skiing, soccer, swimming, tennis, track and field [both indoor and outdoor], volleyball, crew and squash), men's participation average total is 347.9 and the women's participation average is 274.6. Yet more grants are available to women in these sports than to men. Nonetheless, men represent 56 percent of the participants and women represent 44 percent. Would this meet the strict proportionality test if a student body was 50 percent male and 50 percent female? It is even more onerous if the female student body is greater than 50 percent. It definitely would not meet OCR's compliance test and demonstrates the absurdity of strict proportionality.

Let us cite a specific example. The University of North Carolina at Chapel Hill was awarded last year's Sears Directors Cup that recognizes an institution's athletic achievement by combining the success of its men's and women's sports programs. The University of North Carolina at Chapel Hill currently has an enrollment of 42 percent male and 58 percent female. It sponsors 13 sports for women and will add a fourteenth sport for women next year. Women's sports do not lack for funding at the University of North Carolina. The institution also sponsors 13 sports for men. The participation rate in the athletic department, however, is almost the reverse of the gender enrollment of the student body with more than 50 percent of the participants being male. Who is to say that the University of North Carolina is not providing adequate competitive opportunities for all students on the campus, both male and female?

Some advocates of women's athletics have stated publicly that a method to achieve strict proportionality would be to reduce opportunities for men. They would eliminate those that wish to try out for a team, what we refer to as walk-ons. Because women do not try out in the same numbers their ill-founded solution is to eliminate opportunities for men and that is not the American way. Many of those that walk on do not make the final squad. Some, however, become outstanding athletes and major contributors to the university, as many coaches will testify.

Let us consider proportionality at the Division III level. Central College of Pella, Iowa has long had a successful football program. Central College is proud of the fact that of a student enrollment of 1,400, of which approximately 55 percent is female, there are 125 members on the football squad. At the Division III level, those that are attending college pay their own way. There are no athletic grants-in-aid. The reason that they are on the football squad is that they want an opportunity to play the game. Should Central College be required to limit the number that want to play football because of a strict proportionality test?

Those who attack football concentrate primarily on those institutions that sponsor the sport at the highest competitive level, Division I-A. In doing so, they question the need for a specific number of grants-in-aid with the expectation that if such numbers were reduced, the money should automatically go to women's sports. This attack is unfair, unfounded and not in the best interest of women's sports. Look at the current Sears Director's Cup standings that reflect institutions having achieved success in athletics for both men and women. Without exception the highest rated programs are associated with universities that also offer football at the Division I-A level. The fact is that the most prominent and best funded women's athletic programs benefit because those universities also sponsor major college football. That fact should demonstrate above all else that football, despite its size and because of its popularity, does aid women's sports.

I find it difficult to believe that the sponsors of Title IX, in their desire to promote opportunities for women's education, including athletics, intended to hurt football or eliminate opportunities for men. Although Title IX is an educational act, the focus on strict proportionality rests solely on athletics and there is no investigation about the percentage of females enrolled in business or engineering or males enrolled in nursing or education. In fact, Senator Bayh, the Senate sponsor of Title IX is quoted from the Congressional Record August 6, 1971 as stating, "What we are trying to do is provide *equal access* for women and men to the educational process and the extracurricular activities in a school, where there is not a unique facet such as football involved."

Let me reiterate what I said earlier:

1. We are not asking football to be exempt from Title IX.

2. The unique size of the sport of football must be taken into consideration. This is what the Policy Interpretations promised but failed to deliver.

3. If participation in sports is good for men, it must also be good for women. Hopefully there will be opportunities available to both.

4. We seek practical interpretations and guidelines relative to Title IX. The current Policy Interpretation needs to be revisited because it is outdated and lacks the necessary clarification by the agency that is responsible to interpret it . . . OCR

Finally, do not make those colleges and universities that sponsor football prisoners of strict proportionality.

APPENDIX A

Fact Sheet: UNEU and Newtown, Massachusetts[1]

Enrollment: 10,000 students

Full-time undergraduate student tuition: $10,252

Full-time undergraduate student fees: $379

Room and board: $2,432

Total: $13,063[2]

Percentage of student body by gender: male, 44 percent, women, 56 percent3,

Population of Newtown: 85,000 (plus 10,000 students when school is in session).

Sports Teams

MEN'S TEAMS	PARTICIPANTS	5-YEAR AGGREGATE GPA[4]	WOMEN'S TEAMS	PARTICIPANTS	5-YEAR AGGREGATE GPA	YEAR ADDED
Football	115 (85 scholarships, 30 walk-ons)	2.5	Crew	50	N/A	1975
Basketball	15	2.5	Basketball	15	2.85	Before Title IX
Soccer	25	2.9	Soccer	25	3.17	Before Title IX
Golf	10	3.0	Golf	10	3.2	1975
Swimming	10	2.9	Field hockey	35	3.15	1975
Volleyball	15	3.0	Volleyball	15	3.1	Before Title IX
Lacrosse	25	2.8	Lacrosse	25	3.05	1985
Track and field	25	N/A	Track and field	40	N/A	Before Title IX
Hockey	25	2.9	Bowling	25	2.9	1988
Baseball	30	2.8	Softball	25	3.05	1975
Wrestling	20	2.65				
Total: 11	315		Total: 10	265		

Racial Distribution

- Of overall student population: 75 percent white, 10 percent African American, 8 percent Hispanic, 7 percent other

- Of male athletes: 64.4 percent white, 23 percent African American, 12.6 percent other

- Of female athletes: 72 percent white, 14 percent African American, 14 percent other (if you eliminate basketball and track and field, the figures are 80 percent white, 6 percent African American, and 14 percent other)

UNEU has not administered any survey of students to determine whether it is meeting women's desire to participate in intercollegiate athletics.

APPENDIX B

Abbreviations

AD Athletic Director
AIAW Association for Intercollegiate Athletics for Women
GM Gamemaster
HEW Department of Health, Education, and Welfare
NCAA National Collegiate Athletics Association
OCR Office of Civil Rights
PIPs Personal Influence Points

SELECTED BIBLIOGRAPHY

Works about Women's sports and Title IX

Cahn, Susan. *Coming on Strong: Gender and Sexuality in Women's Sports.* New York: Free Press, 1994.

Gavora, Jessica. *Tilting the Playing Field: Title IX, Schools, Sports, Sex and Title IX.* New York: Encounter Books, 2003.

Hogshead-Makar, Nancy. *Equal Play: Title IX and Social Change.* Philadelphia, PA: Temple University Press, 2007.

Mitchell, Nicole. *Encyclopedia of Title IX and Sports.* Santa Barbara, CA: Greenwood, 2007.

O'Reilly, Jean, and Susan Cahn. *Women in Sports: A Documentary Reader.* Lebanon, NH: Northeastern University Press, 2007.

Parks, Janet B. *Title IX: Implications for Women in Sport and Education.* 2009; Bowling Green, OH: WBGU-TV. DVD.

Simon, Rita, ed. *Sporting Equality: Title IX Thirty Years Later.* New Brunswick, NJ: Transaction Publishers, 2005.

Suggs, Welch. *A Place on the Team: The Triumph and Tragedy of Title IX.* Princeton, NJ: Princeton University Press, 2006.

Background Texts about the History of Sports in the United States

Clotfelter, Charles. *Big-Time Sports in American Universities.* Cambridge: Cambridge University Press, 2011.

Davies, Richard O. *Sports in American Life: A History.* 2nd ed. Hoboken, NJ: Wiley-Blackwell, 2012.

Jay, Kathryn. *More Than Just a Game: Sports in American Life since 1945.* New York: Columbia University Press, 2006.

Roberts, Randy. *Winning Is the Only Thing: Sports in America since 1945.* Baltimore, MD: John Hopkins University Press, 1991.

Riess, Steven A., and Thomas Paterson, eds. *Major Problems in American Sports History.* Boston: Houghton-Mifflin, 1996.

Smith, Ronald. *Sports and Freedom: The Rise of Big-Time College Athletics.* New York: Oxford University Press, 1990.

NOTES

Part 1: Introduction

1. This fictional university is a composite of several colleges and universities that experienced conflict at that time over enforcing Title IX requirements. These include Brown University, the University of Illinois, Marquette University, Miami University (of Ohio), and Western Illinois University.

Part 2: Historical Background

1. Stefan Szymanski, "A Theory of the Evolution of Modern Sport," *Journal of Sport History* 35 (2008): 2.

2. These British "public" schools of the nineteenth century were, in fact, quite exclusive, akin to the elite private schools of today.

3. C. Roger Rees and Andrew W. Miracle, "Education and Sport," in *Handbook of Sports Studies*, ed. Jay Coakley and Eric Dunning (Thousand Oaks, CA: Sage Publications, 2000), p. 278.

4. Jean O'Reilly and Susan Cahn, eds., *Women and Sport in the United States* (Boston: Northeastern University Press, 2007), p. xiii.

5. For more on the history of women's cycling clothing, see the Bikes & Bloomers Project, May 27, 2019, http://bikesandbloomers.com.

6. Hilary Levey Friedman, "When Did Competitive Sports Take over American Childhood?" *Atlantic*, September 20, 2013, accessed May 27, 1019, www.theatlantic.com/education/archive/2013/09/when-did-competitive-sports-take-over-american-childhood/279868.

7. O'Reilly and Cahn, *Women and Sport in the United States*, p. xiv.

8. Richard Bell, "A History of Women in Sport Prior to Title IX," *Sport Journal* 10 (2007): 1, http://thesportjournal.org/article/a-history-of-women-in-sport-prior-to-title-ix.

9. O'Reilly and Cahn, *Women and Sport in the United States*, p. xiv.

10. O'Reilly and Cahn, *Women and Sport in the United States*, p. xv.

11. "Looking Back: The First Game," 125 Stanford Stories, no. 32, accessed January 10, 2019, https://125.stanford.edu/the-first-game.

12. Bell, "A History of Women in Sport Prior to Title IX."

13. Frederick Rudolph, "The Rise of Football," in *The American College and University: A History* (New York: Knopf, 1962), pp. 374–75.

14. Rodney Smith, "Little Ado about Something: Playing the Game with the Reform of Big-Time Athletics," *Capital University Law Review* 20 (1991): 570.

15. Howard J. Savage, Harold Bentley, John T. McGovern, Dean F. Smiley, *American College Athletics*, Bull. 23 (New York: Carnegie Foundation for the Advancement of Teaching, 1929), excerpt accessed May 28, 2019, www.thecoia.org/wp-content/uploads/2014/09/Carnegie-Commission-1929-excerpts-1.pdf.

16. Friedman, "When Did Competitive Sports Take over American Childhood?"

17. Jeff Leen, *Queen of the Ring: Sex, Muscles, Diamonds, and the Making of an American Legend* (New York: Atlantic Monthly Press, 2009).

18. Varda Burstyn, *The Rites of Men: Manhood, Politics, and the Culture of Sport* (Toronto: University of Toronto Press, 1999).

19. Amby Burfoot, "First Lady of Boston," *Runners World*, April 6, 2016, www.runnersworld.com/races-places/a20791759/first-lady-of-boston.

20. "Immaculata, Queens College to Play," *ESPN*, September 19, 2014, accessed September 23, 2019, https://www.espn.com/womens-college-basketball/story/_/id/11552315/immaculata-queens-college-celebrate-40th-anniversary-matchup-maggie-dixon-classic.

21. See the section "Distributive Justice: Toward a Theory of Compliance" (later in the game book) for more on equity vs. parity.

22. Andy Schwartz, "The NCAA Isn't Going Broke, No Matter How Much You Hear It," FiveThirtyEight, ABC News, April 20, 2018, https://fivethirtyeight.com/features/the-ncaa-isnt-going-broke-no-matter-how-much-you-hear-it.

23. In 1973, the NCAA rescinded its formal prohibition of female student-athletes competing in NCAA championship events.

24. Daniel Marburger and Nancy Hogshead-Makar, "Is Title IX Really to Blame for the Decline in Intercollegiate Men's Nonrevenue Sports," *Marquette Sport Law Review* 14 (2003–2004): 65.

25. Chris Armstrong, *Global Distributive Justice: An Introduction* (New York: Cambridge University Press, 2012), p. 16.

26. Michelle Maiese, "Distributive Justice," Beyond Intractability, Conflict Information Consortium, University of Colorado, Boulder, updated June 2013 by Heidi Burgess, www.beyondintractability.org/essay/distributive-justice.

27. Leslie Francis, "Title IX: Equality for Women's Sports?" *Journal of the Philosophy of Sport* 20–21 (1993–1994): 37.

28. Robert L. Simon, Cesar R. Torres, and Peter F. Hager, *Fair Play: The Ethics of Sport* (Boulder, CO: Westview Press, 2014), p. 145.

29. Robert Simon, "Gender Equity and Inequity in Athletics," *Journal of the Philosophy of Sport* 20–21 (1993–1994): 7.

30. Francis, "Title IX," 44.

31. Some state-sponsored universities report to a state-level board, sometimes elected, sometimes appointed, that runs the entire state system of public institutions. As a private (not state-supported or sponsored) school, this isn't relevant for UNEU.

32. A few additional notes of clarification: First, conferences (the Big Ten, for instance) have complicated agreements by which members share some kinds of income—for example, money made from postseason play. Second, student-athletes throughout the NCAA sign agreements when they arrive on campus giving their university and the NCAA the exclusive right to license their name and image to people who make video games, highlight films, T-shirts, bobblehead dolls, and so on. These agreements are often in perpetuity, meaning that even twenty-five years after the athlete graduates, the NCAA is still the only organization able to make money off his or her image or name.

33. At schools where tickets (usually for football or basketball) are in high demand, universities will often require nonstudents who want to buy tickets to pay an upfront donation of money to the university before purchasing tickets. This may be as high as several thousand dollars. I put the phrase *personal seat license* in quotes because universities don't actually call it this. That is, however, what it is: a fee that offers you the right to purchase tickets.

34. According to a 2002 study, only 35 percent of Division 1A (the NCAA division that includes the largest universities) athletic departments made money in the 2000–2001 fiscal year. See Brian Porto, *A New Season: Using Title IX to Reform College Sports* (Westport, Praeger, 2003), p. 52.

35. Porto, *A New Season*, p. 53.

36. As of 2018, very recent changes will allow some universities to pay athletes a stipend in addition to their expenses. It is unclear at this point how often UNEU will take advantage of this option.

37. This is the NCAA maximum time a student-athlete is allowed to practice with his or her team supervised by a coach. There are many exceptions to this rule. And it is clear that many athletes in reality spend more than forty hours a week participating in athletic activities, whether that means watching film or lifting weights or shooting free throws in a gym by himself or herself.

38. The Scholarship Stats website offers a good summary of scholarship limits and terms: "College Athletic Scholarship Limits," accessed April 16, 2019, www.reachhighscholars.org /Articles/College%20Athletic%20Scholarship %20Limits.pdf.

39. The only real comparison to this is among medical doctors, for many of the same historical and professional reasons. It's not really far off to imagine a university as a fancy medical clinic. For those who know something about European history, the universities and medical clinics are among the very few institutions left that aren't really jobs at all but rather guilds.

Part 3: The Game

1. See Richard O. Davies, *Sports in American Life: A History*, 2nd ed. (Hoboken, NJ: Wiley-Blackwell, 2012), chap. 3.

2. *Forbes* magazine estimated that the University of Alabama football team was worth $92 million in 2009. Its coach, Nick Saban, earned $4 million in salary that same year. In comparison, the university paid Bear Bryant, who coached in the middle of the twentieth century, an estimated $17,500 for his first year coaching Alabama (in 2009 dollars, just under $130,000). Neither of these figures includes income earned from nonuniversity employers. Peter Schwartz, "College Football's Most Valuable Teams," *Forbes*, December 22, 2009, www.forbes.com/2009/12/22/most-vaulable -college-football-teams-business-sports -college-football.html; and Charles Land, "Bryant Signs 10-Year Pact As Coach for Crimson Tide," *Tuscaloosa News*, December 3, 1957, p. 1.

3. Symbolically, you can understand this as having used your influence to get a friend of yours, who respects you and will vote the way you wish, appointed to the Board.

Appendix A

1. Linda Carpenter and R. Vivian Acosta compile a yearly report on women's participation in sports. These data are drawn from a number of these yearly studies. See www.acostacarpenter .org, accessed November 3, 2014.

2. These prices are the approximate costs for Creighton University in 1994, a reasonable approximation for UNEU. For comparison, the total cost to attend Creighton in 2014 is approximately $45,258 (before financial aid). See www.collegesimply.com/colleges/nebraska /creighton-university/price/#.U8_hoPld-VbE, accessed July 23, 2014.

3. See https://nces.ed.gov/programs/digest/d96 /d96t171.asp, accessed November 16, 2013.

4. Both GPA columns drawn loosely from aggregate data provided in Brianna M. Scott, Thomas S. Paskus, Michael Miranda, and Todd A. Petr, "In-Season vs. Out-of-Season Academic Performance of College Student-Athletes," *Journal of Intercollegiate Sports* 1 (2008): 202–226. I've simply taken approximations from the aggregate data for Division 1 schools and applied them to UNEU. The data are counterfactual in the sense that they are from the first decade of the twenty-first century, but should be good enough for the purposes of the game. N/A signals not available.

CREDITS

Text

Acosta, R. Vivian and Linda Jean Carpenter: From "Women in Intercollegiate Sport: A Longitudinal, National Study, Thirty-Seven Year Update," 2014. © 2014 Acosta/Carpenter. Reprinted by permission of the authors.

All-American Girls Professional Baseball League: "The Rules of Conduct for Players as Set up by the All-American Girls Professional Baseball League," reprinted by permission of the Northern Indiana Historical Society.

Feigen, Brenda: From "Giving Women a Sporting Chance," *Ms. Magazine*, July 1973, pp. 56–58, 103. Reprinted by permission of the author.

Gavora, Jessica: "How Women Beat Men at College Sports," *The Women's Quarterly*, Autumn 1995, pp. 4–5. Originally published by the Independent Women's Forum. Reprinted with permission.

Gilbert, Bil and Nancy Williamson: "Sport Is Unfair to Women (Part 1)," *Sports Illustrated*, May 28, 1973, pp. 88–98. Reprinted by permission of the authors' estates.

Miller, Heather Ross: "Half-Court Basketball: Power & Sex," *Witness*, Vol. 6, No. 2, 1992. Copyright © 1992 Witness. Reprinted by permission of Witness Magazine and Heather Ross Miller.

National Organization for Women: "The National Organization for Women's 1966 Statement of Purpose," by Betty Friedan. Reprinted with permission of National Organization for Women. This is a historical document and may not reflect the current language or priorities of the organization.

Photo

Page 17: Library of Congress.

ACKNOWLEDGMENTS

While writing seems like a solitary activity, it is actually the distillation of dozens of conversations, suggestions, referrals, and favors. *Changing the Game* wouldn't exist without the help of hundreds of colleagues and students who offered their time, attention, and listening ears. In particular, we'd like to thank Nick Proctor, Jace Weaver, Mark Higbee, and the others who, at the Game Development Conference at Central Michigan University, imagined a way to reframe the game that instantly made it both more meaningful and much more fun. Thanks go as well to the entire Reacting community, including Mark Carnes, Jenn Worth, Madelena Provo, the members of the Reacting Editorial Board, and Mark Higbee, Naomi Norman, and Gretchen Galbraith, each of whom generously offered up their institutions for early playtests. Justin Cahill, Rachel Taylor, Funto Omojola, Angie Merila, and their colleagues at Norton were wonderful to work with as well.

At Newman, Kelly McFall would like to thank the professional development committee as well as Mike Austin and Kim Long for supporting countless requests for resources. Vic Trilli and Joanna Pryor answered question after question about how athletic departments work. Steve Hamersky, Jeanette Parker, and Emily Simon together make up the best library staff in the country. Thanks to them for endless hours spent searching for obscure sources and helping me navigate the far reaches of the web. Hundreds of students at Newman played the game and offered useful feedback. It should not diminish the contributions of others to single out Emily Simon and Jaimie (Dungan) Fager (again), Erin Mink, Leanne Vastbinder, Lauren Spencer, and Linnea Ristow for particularly important suggestions. Finally, as always, thanks to Laura, Jenna, and Emily for their gifts of time and love. I have no life: my kids row crew and play softball. May they always have the chance to do so.

Abby Perkiss extends a debt of gratitude to her colleagues in the history department at Kean University for their support of *Reacting to the Past*, and to her intrepid students, who enthusiastically guinea-pigged *Title IX* and offered thoughtful and constructive feedback with each playtest. My thanks, too, to Kelly McFall, who brought the idea of this game to the GDC in 2012 and invited me on as a collaborator, and to the broader Reacting community for supporting the development of this project and offering Kelly and me opportunities to test and hone the game over the last several years. Thanks to my mom, who grew up in the last pre-Title IX generation and instilled in me from a young age just how revolutionary the law was, and to my dad, who drove me to every swim practice and volunteered at every meet for over a decade. Thanks to Brent—my teammate and husband. Brent and I have raced alongside each other all over the world, from Atlantic storms in Ireland, to sleepmonsters in Tasmania, to the top of the podium at the national championship. There's no one I'd rather adventure with. To Zoe, and now Simon, for supporting us in having identities beyond that of parents (and to their grandparents and aunts for standing *in loco parentis* better than we could have imagined). Finally, thanks to all the women who challenged the status quo and staked their claim in sports; I've been a competitive athlete most of my life, and I'm endlessly indebted to them for creating a world where I didn't have to wage that fight.